30.50

369 0289463

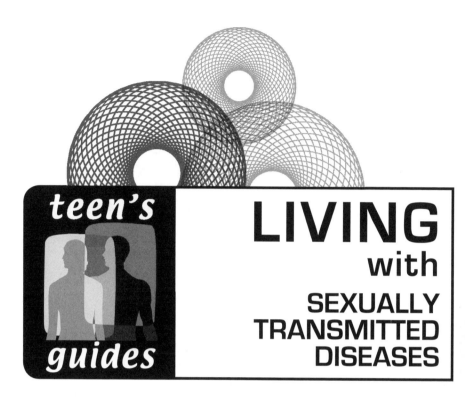

teen's guides

LIVING
with
SEXUALLY
TRANSMITTED
DISEASES

Also in the
Teen's Guides series

teen's guides

LIVING
with
SEXUALLY TRANSMITTED DISEASES

Carol A. Ford, M.D.
with Elizabeth Shimer Bowers

Facts On File
An imprint of Infobase Publishing

Living with Sexually Transmitted Diseases

Facts On File, Inc.
An imprint of Infobase Publishing, Inc.
132 West 31st Street
New York NY 10001

A Cataloging in Publication record is available from the Library of Congress
ISBN-13: 978-0-8160-7672-7
ISBN-10: 0-8160-7672-3

Facts On File books are available at special discounts when purchased in bulk quantities for businesses, associations, institutions, or sales promotions. Please call our Special Sales Department in New York at (212) 967-8800 or (800) 322-8755. You can find Facts On File on the World Wide Web at http://www.factsonfile.com

Text design by Annie O'Donnell
Cover design by Jooyoung An

Printed in the United States of America

MP MSRF 10 9 8 7 6 5 4 3 2 1

This book is printed on acid-free paper.

Disclaimer: The information provided in this book is designed to help you make informed decisions about your sexual health. It is not intended to be used as a substitute for any advice or treatments from your doctor. If you suspect you may have a sexually transmitted disease, see your doctor right away. Science and medicine can change rapidly. New research leads to increased understanding of sexually transmitted diseases and to new recommendations for prevention, diagnosis, and treatment of infections. The authors have reviewed sources believed to be reliable in their efforts to provide information that is complete and in accord with professional standards acceptable during the writing of this book. However, since there is possibility of human error and changes in medical science, the authors cannot claim that all information in this book is in every respect accurate and complete and disclaim all responsibility for any errors or omissions or for the results obtained from use of information in this book. Readers are encouraged to confirm information obtained in this book with other sources.

CONTENTS

Preface:
A Note to Parents

Most parents do not want their teenagers to have sex. Many adults believe that teenagers are too young to have sex, because of family values, health concerns, or both. Nonetheless, despite the best wishes of parents and other adults, the vast majority of teenagers have had sex before the age of 20. Some begin having sex as early as middle school, and a substantial number begin having sex in high school.

Teenagers who have sex are at very high risk of acquiring sexually transmitted diseases (STDs). In March of 2008 the Centers for Disease Control and Prevention released the results of a national study estimating that one in four (26 percent) young women in the United States between 14 and 19 years of age has an STD. This is unacceptably high.

To reduce STD rates among teenagers, multiple strategies are needed. One important strategy is to delay the onset of first sex. Teenagers who do not have sexual exposure to infections do not get STDs.

Among teenagers who do have sex, important strategies to reduce STDs include consistent correct condom use, limiting their number of sexual partners, and visiting a doctor or nurse at least once a year to be tested for silent STDs. There are also new vaccines to prevent STDs, which are most effective when a person is vaccinated before having sex. This book is written to provide teenagers with information about all of these STD-prevention strategies.

It is not easy to write a book for teenagers about STDs because there are dramatic differences between teenagers in early, middle, and late adolescence. The information one specific teenager needs to avoid STDs will change according to where he or she is in his or her own adolescence, romantic relationships, and sexual behaviors. This book is meant to be respectful of such complexity while also providing the basic facts to all teenagers who might read it. There is no evidence that providing honest, factual information about sex and STDs to adolescents causes harm. Teaching adolescents about prevention, diagnosis, and treatment of STDs does not increase their likelihood of having sex or risky sex; it simply provides information that will be useful if and when they ever have sex. This book is not meant to be a replacement for regular conversations between teenagers, parents, and health care professionals, but rather a supplement to or perhaps a stimulus for those conversations.

Ready or Not? Sex and Its Possible Consequences

Kathy, age 16, can't decide whether or not she should have sex. Her boyfriend Seth has been putting pressure on her recently, and she is afraid that if she says no, she will disappoint Seth or risk losing him. But Kathy is not sure that having sex at this time in her life is the right thing for her.

Kathy is far from being alone. Many teenagers—both girls and boys—struggle with similar decisions. And it's no surprise—the decision of if and when to have sex is a huge one, and it should not be taken lightly. After you have sex for the first time and "lose your virginity," it is something that you can never change. Many teenagers who decide to have sex later regret it. Some get hurt emotionally. Some get hurt physically. Plus, having sex comes with some enormous responsibilities. You have to deal with the risks of getting a *sexually transmitted disease (STD),* which may or may not be curable. And you must face the risks of you or your partner becoming pregnant. Sex can be a wonderful thing, but teenagers like Kathy need to ask themselves, "Is this the right time in my life for sex? Is this the right person? Is this the right situation? And will having sex compromise the values my parents have taught me?"

A TOUGH DECISION AT A TOUGH TIME

This book is about infections that you can get when you have sex. No one wants to get an STD, and there is only one way to

1

completely avoid getting one—abstain from having sex. Many young people do not have to worry about STDs because they have decided to wait to have sex until they are older. This is a choice that definitely protects their health. But other young people who have opted to have sex *do* have to worry about STDs because getting infected is a very real possibility.

Keep in mind that although the decision of whether or not to have sex for the first time is a big one, it is not just a one-time choice. You will make decisions about whether or not to have sex in your 20s, 30s, 40s, 50s—for the rest of your life, every time a sexual situation develops. So it is important to think carefully about these decisions before you have to make them. This chapter will help teenagers like Kathy—and you, if you are faced with the same decision—make healthy choices when it comes to having sex.

WHAT TO CONSIDER WHEN MAKING THE DECISION OF WHETHER OR NOT TO HAVE SEX

Ultimately, you will have to make the decision of whether or not to have sex yourself; no one can make it for you. These are some of the things you should consider to help you make an informed decision.

Most teens have not had sex. Between all the gossip at school and the sex you see teenagers having in the media, you may feel like everyone around you is engaging in sex. This is not true. Although there may be a lot of talk about it, the vast majority of students in middle school and two-thirds of students in early high school have *not* had sex. Among seniors in high school, 40 percent report that they have not had *sexual intercourse*. And among teenagers who have had sex, some really regret their decisions. Even if your friends and/or siblings are having sex, that doesn't mean it is necessarily the right time for *you*. As difficult as it may be to not let others' decisions regarding sex influence yours, you really need to make the choice for yourself. The only person who can tell you that you are ready for sex is you.

Teens who wait to have sex until they are older generally make healthier choices. Think about all of the choices linked to having sex. Is this the right time in your life? Is this the right person? Is this the right thing for your relationship? Is this something you will regret? If you have sex, will you get hurt emotionally?

If you have sex, how will you protect yourself from STDs? If you have sex, what will happen if you (or your partner) gets pregnant? If you are not ready to become a parent, how will you prevent that from happening? What science tells us is that, in general, older people make safer choices than younger people. You can still make safe choices even if you are young, but it may be a lot easier to do this when you are older. So, it is important to ask yourself, what's the rush? Waiting until you are older may be a very smart thing to do.

Your values are important. Many people base their decision of whether or not to have sex in their teenage years on their moral or religious values. If the values you have developed as a result of your family or church are important to you, think about them carefully, and make a decision that agrees with them. If having sex is in line with these values, you may be ready. If it conflicts with them, on the other hand, you may not. Think about how you will feel after you have sex—will you feel happy and fulfilled, or will you feel guilty? To further help you weigh the moral implications of your decision, you may want to talk to someone you trust, such as a parent, relative, or leader in your church.

You should never be pressured into having sex. Your friends may be talking to you about who's having sex, and asking you when you are planning to do it. Your boyfriend or girlfriend may be putting pressure on you to have sex and threatening to leave the relationship if you don't agree. And you may feel like you are faced with sexual images wherever you turn—on magazine pages, in television commercials, and in movies. You don't have to have sex to please other people. After all, having sex to fit in, impress other people, or to make others happy will not make you feel very good about yourself in the long run.

Someone who loves and cares about you should respect your decisions about sex. Some teenagers let their feelings for a boyfriend or girlfriend cloud their reasoning when it comes to having sex. Keep in mind that real love is not based on sex. People can show their love for each other in many nonsexual ways, including talking, listening, and spending quality time together. Sure, sex can add some wonderful things to the right relationship at the right time in your life, but a person who truly loves you will not stop loving you simply because you choose not to have sex. If your boyfriend or girlfriend threatens breaking up with you if you do not give in to having sexual intercourse, he or she is not worth your time or emotions, and you can be thankful that you didn't have sex with someone who doesn't truly care for or respect you.

Only consider having sex if you are in a healthy relationship. To help analyze your relationship to see if it is healthy, ask yourself the following questions:

▸ Do you and your partner treat each other as equals?
▸ Are you and your partner honest with each other?
▸ Do you trust your partner?
▸ Do you respect your partner's feelings and needs, and do you feel that he or she respects yours?

What to consider when making decisions about sex: a review

1. Most teens have not had sex.

2. Teens who wait to have sex until they are older generally make healthier choices.

3. Your values are important.

4. You should never be pressured into having sex.

5. Making decisions about sex is complicated.

6. Talking to a trusted adult can be extremely helpful.

7. Abstinence (not having sex) is a really healthy choice.

8. If you choose to have sex, you will have to deal with the potential for pregnancy.

9. If you choose to have sex, you will have to deal with the potential for STDs.

10. If you are considering sex, or have had sex, you need to see a doctor or nurse.

- ➤ Do you enjoy each other's company?
- ➤ Do you share similar values and interests?
- ➤ Do you both accept responsibility for things in your lives?
- ➤ Do you protect each other?
- ➤ Do you both feel that now is a good time to have sex?
- ➤ Are you both ready for sex?

If you answered "yes" to all of the above questions, you still need to consider the rest of the factors mentioned in this chapter and in the remainder of the book before you make a final decision about whether to have sex.

Making decisions about sex is complicated. In the midst of puberty, you may be having a lot of sexual urges and thoughts. This is normal—it means your hormones are working properly. But curiosity about sex and feeling like you are physically ready should not be confused with emotional readiness to do it; after all, the emotional readiness is the most important part. You may not understand how sex will affect you emotionally, and you could face confusion, shame, and angst if you make the wrong decision in the heat of the moment.

Complex emotions related to sex are common. Sex can be pleasurable, or it can be uncomfortable and humiliating. Having sex may make you feel mature and empowered, or it could make you feel shameful or guilty. As you struggle with the decision of whether or not to have sex, you may feel curious about the physical and emotional feelings it will stir in you. You may be afraid to resist your partner's requests for sex. You may also feel embarrassed because you are not confident in the appearance of your body.

If you are leaning toward having sex, what are your reasons? Are you thinking about having sex simply to satisfy your curiosity or to have casual fun? Are you thinking about having sex mainly because you are sad or lonely? Are you afraid that if you do not have sex your partner will stop loving you or leave you? What are your partner's reasons for wanting to have sex? If you are thinking about having sex, make sure you do not have it for the wrong reasons. Sex has many consequences, so the decision of whether or not to have it should not be taken lightly.

If you do not want to have sex, how far will you go? Having sex means different things to different people. Think hard about your limits and about what you are truly ready for. Clearly communicate your decision to your boyfriend or girlfriend. And remember that there are some "sexual" activities that carry almost no risk of STDs, including hugging and holding hands.

Talking to a trusted adult can be extremely helpful. When making the decision of whether or not to have sex, consider talking to your mom or dad. Many parents will support their children in being responsible for their decisions, even if they don't necessarily agree with them. If you're not comfortable talking to a parent about sex, talk to another adult. Think of the adults in your life who care about you and want to help. Teenagers sometimes talk to their grandparents, an aunt or uncle, an older cousin, a teacher or counselor at school, or their friend's mom or dad. You can also go talk to a doctor or nurse. The bottom line is that talking with an adult, and going to an adult for help when you need it, is a whole lot better than dealing with complicated issues like sex, preventing pregnancy, and STDs alone.

If you choose to talk to your parents about sex, the way you approach the topic will make a difference in the comfort level of everyone involved. Here are some tips on how to make the conversation go smoothly:

▸ Make sure it is a good time. If your parents come home exhausted after a hard day, they are not in good moods, or they are busy, find a better time. You may tell them you have something to discuss with them ahead of time, and ask them when would be a good time to talk.

▸ Ease your parents into the conversation. Instead of blurting out, "I'm thinking about having sex with Jim," say something like, "Do you think people should wait until they're married to have sex?"

▸ Use a book, an article, or a TV show to break the ice. Say something like, "I ran across this article, and I am curious to hear what you think about it."

▸ Listen to your parents' response. They will be much more likely to help you if you listen to what they have to say.

▸ Try not to yell or argue. Conflict will only make the situation uncomfortable and tense. Remember: you might disagree with your parents, but you should respect them.

▸ If your parents become judgmental or start lecturing, remind them that you're just asking questions. Tell them you want to be open and honest with them, and that you also value their opinions.

Abstinence (not having sex) is a really healthy choice. Many teens think long and hard about what it means to have sex, and they ultimately decide to forgo having sex until they are older and more mature. These teens have a variety of reasons for choosing *abstinence*. Some feel that having sex conflicts with their moral or religious values. Some don't want to worry about unplanned pregnancy or the possibility of getting an STD. And other teens recognize that they are not emotionally ready to handle sex, and they want to wait until they are absolutely sure that they are.

Once you have made your decision, you will have to discuss it with your partner and be clear about your feelings toward sex. If your decision is "no," be prepared for a protest, just in case, and don't feel at all bad about sticking to your decision. To avoid surprising your partner with your decision, don't just spring it on him or her on a whim. Instead, tell him or her ahead of time that you have something you want to talk about. Make sure that the two of you are in a place where you have privacy and can talk freely. If your decision is "yes," keep in mind that you can change your mind at any point, even right before you are about to have sex.

If you have decided against having sex and you feel that your partner is not giving you the respect you deserve, it may be time for you to take a good hard look at your relationship. A lack of respect for such an important decision is not a sign of a good, healthy, supportive relationship. The bottom line is that if you don't feel respected and supported, it may be time for you to get out of the relationship.

If you choose to have sex, you will have to deal with the potential for pregnancy. Recognize that pregnancy is a possibility *every time* a male and female have vaginal intercourse unless they take actions to prevent it. Preventing unwanted pregnancy is the responsibility of both people involved. If you are going to have sex, using a condom is imperative—this protects against both pregnancy and STDs. Adding a regular method of hormonal contraception (for example, *birth control pills* or shots) gives you the most protection. You also need to know about emergency contraception and how to get it if you need it. These are all issues you should think about and discuss with your partner *before* you decide to have sex.

The basics of prevention of unwanted pregnancy are as follows:

▸ Abstinence is the only completely guaranteed way to prevent pregnancy.
▸ The two main ways that teenagers who have sex can prevent pregnancy are by using hormonal contraception and condoms.
▸ For hormonal contraception, most teenagers choose birth control pills, patches, or Depo-Provera shots, which are all prescribed by a doctor. They work to prevent the egg from leaving the ovary (ovulation), and they change the mucus in the *vagina* to make it too thick for sperm to move through. Birth control pills are taken by mouth once per day, patches are placed on the skin once a week, and Depo-Provera shots involve injections in the woman's buttocks or arm every three months. Although all of these methods prevent pregnancy 99 percent of the time when used properly, they do not prevent STDs.
▸ Condoms are a barrier method of birth control. They provide a physical blockade to prevent the sperm from getting to the egg. Condoms are the most effective method for preventing STDs, but they are not as effective as hormonal methods for preventing pregnancy. *Male condoms* are available in drugstores, and they are rolled onto the man's erect *penis* right before sex.
▸ **If you have sex, the safest way to prevent pregnancy and STDs is for female partners to use hormonal contraception (pills, patches, or shots) AND for male partners to wear a condom each time you have sex.**
▸ One birth control method attempted by some teenagers—which is NOT effective and therefore should not be used—is the withdrawal method. During the withdrawal method, the male pulls his penis out of his partner's vagina before he ejaculates. This is NOT a good method for preventing STDs because it involves no barriers, and it is not effective for preventing pregnancy. Sperm are in the drops of semen that come out of the penis early during sex, before ejaculation. And it is very difficult for men to pull out "at the right time."
▸ Every person who has sex should know about emergency contraception. If you and your partner have sex without a condom or the condom breaks, and the female partner is not

on hormonal contraception, you should consider emergency contraception if you do not want to get pregnant. Emergency contraception involves taking pills by mouth within five days of unprotected sex, but the sooner you take it, the more effective it is. Emergency contraception is a safe and simple way to dramatically reduce your chances of getting pregnant in this "emergency" situation. In many states, if you are at least 17 years of age, you can get emergency contraception without a prescription from a pharmacy. If you are under age 18 and are relying on condoms for birth control, consider asking your doctor or nurse to write you a prescription for emergency contraception just in case you need it. If you need emergency contraception immediately, you can call your doctor or nurse, go to a clinic or emergency room, or call Planned Parenthood. Emergency contraception does not protect against STDs.

You should also have an idea of what you will do if you or your partner becomes pregnant. Is *abortion* an option for you? What are your partner's opinions on abortion? Will you consider adoption? What are your partner's opinions on adoption? If you do decide to have the baby, will you be able to care for it yourself? Where will you live, and who will you live with? Will you be able to afford all of the costs of having a baby and raising a child? How will having a child influence the things that you are currently doing or planning—like school and spending time with friends? Do you have enough friends and relatives who are willing and able to help you raise the child? Do you feel confident that your partner will support you? Do you think he or she will make a good parent? You should consider all these issues before you make the decision of whether or not to have sex.

If you choose to have sex, you will have to deal with the potential for STDs. If you choose to have sex, you may get an STD. There is no way you can be 100 percent sure that you will not get an infection. But if you do choose to have sex, there are four things that dramatically reduce your chances of STDs.

First, you and your partner need to be sure to correctly use latex condoms every time you have sex.

Second, you need to limit your number of partners. If you have sex with only one person, who is only having sex with you, and no one has an infection at the beginning of the relationship, you will reduce your chances of STDs. Every time you have sex with a new person, you expose yourself to more chances of getting an infection. If you are having sex with more than one partner, you really increase your chances of STDs. If you have one partner, break up and have sex with another partner, and then break up and have sex with yet another partner, you will really increase your chances of STDs.

Third, get any vaccines or shots that can protect you from STDs. For example, all teenagers should have had three shots to protect themselves from *Hepatitis B.* And now there are shots to protect girls from getting the types of *human papillomavirus* (HPV) that cause genital warts and cervical cancer. It is best to get these shots

Don't Be Fooled

"I don't want to see my doctor about these symptoms. It would be too embarrassing for both of us."
No matter if you go to the doctor before you have sexual intercourse for the first time or when you are experiencing symptoms of a possible STD, you will probably feel some embarrassment about bringing up the topic during your appointment. But remember: research has shown that when young patients discuss their sexual health with their health care professionals, those patients will be less likely to engage in risky sexual behavior, and therefore, to contract STDs. After all, doctors have the best information when it comes to preventing both STDs and pregnancy, and they will pass that information on to you. Here are some things to keep in mind to help you get over the embarrassment you feel:

Your doctor is there to help you. He or she is not there to judge or punish. If you have had the same family doctor since you were a kid, you may worry that he or she will be disappointed in you for having or thinking of having sex. The main concern of your doctor, however, is to keep you healthy. Period. He or she has probably talked to hundreds of teens who have had or who are thinking about having sexual intercourse, so it should not faze him or her. The role of *before* you have sex, but it is just as important to go get them even if you have already had sex.

Fourth, all adolescents and young adults up to 25 years of age who have ever had sex need to go see a doctor or nurse every year to discuss STD testing, even if you feel well and are not having any problems. This is because most STDs are silent, which means you can be infected and have no way of knowing it. The tests the doctor or nurse recommends will vary based on whether you are a female or male and your sexual history. At the present time, the Centers for Disease Control and Prevention (CDC) recommends that all females who have had sex and are under age 26 be tested for *chlamydia* at least once a year; in some parts of the country,

your doctor is to listen, examine, educate, and treat you, not to judge or criticize.

Your doctor has seen or heard it before. No matter how embarrassed you are about some of your questions or concerns regarding your sexuality or about your actual symptoms, your doctor has probably dealt with worse. So don't feel "gross" or hold anything back.

It's your responsibility to discuss your concerns about sex openly. Your doctor cannot properly treat you if he or she doesn't have the full story. So the more you can verbalize your thoughts, fears, and experiences with sex, the better care you will receive. If you have trouble putting your concerns into words, prepare a written list prior to your appointment, and go over the issues with your doctor one by one. Once you start talking, you will be surprised at how comfortable you feel.

If you cannot express your feelings or symptoms openly and honestly with your doctor because he or she seems uncomfortable or avoids your questions, it is probably time for you to find a new health care provider. As a patient, you have the right to a health care professional who helps you feel comfortable and at ease.

they should also be tested for *gonorrhea.* Three years after first sex, all females should start having regular cervical cytology or *Pap smears.* Recommendations for males are not as consistent as for females, but many health care professionals suggest that they also be tested for chlamydia at least once a year. For both females and males, the CDC also regularly updates recommendations for HIV and *syphilis* testing. The bottom line is that after you have sex, you should talk to a doctor once a year about being tested for silent STDs. **As an important note, there is some wonderful news about STD testing! Some tests that used to require a pelvic examination for females, or a swab in the urethra for males, can now be done on a simple urine test. Getting tested is getting easier all the time!**

If you are considering sex, or have had sex, you need to see a doctor or nurse. If you are thinking about having sex, first, both you and your partner should go for health care. At this visit with your doctor, you will get a check of your general physical health and have the opportunity to talk about prevention of pregnancy and STDs. If you are going to have sex and want to avoid pregnancy and STDs, the safest strategy is for the female to be prescribed hormonal contraception and the male to use condoms every time. If you cannot go to the doctor before you have intercourse, you should go as soon as possible after you start having sex.

And as mentioned above, if you have ever had sex, you need to see a doctor at least once a year to be tested for silent STDs. Of course, if there is a possibility that you may have been exposed to an STD or if you have symptoms of an STD (painful urination, itching, abnormal discharge, abdominal pain, or unusual bumps or rashes or sores), see a doctor right away.

PARENTAL INVOLVEMENT

It is wonderful when teenagers and their parents can discuss decisions about whether or not to have sex, and about prevention of pregnancy and STDs. These conversations are important, even if sometimes difficult. Many parents take their sons and daughters to see a doctor or nurse to get help with issues related to sexuality, or they encourage them to go. But some teenagers and parents find it extraordinarily difficult, or even impossible, to openly discuss issues related to sex. When some teenagers start thinking about going to the doctor for sex-related issues, one of the first questions that many of them ask is, "do my parents have to know?!"

Ideally, your regular doctor has been working with you and your parents to help you learn how to take an increasing amount of responsibility for your health and health care during adolescence. Ideally, he or she has been spending part of each visit with you privately and has been offering to help you make healthy decisions in regards to sex and prevention of pregnancy and STDs. In general, the developmental process is that parents have more direct involvement in teenagers' health care during early adolescence and less direct involvement during middle to late adolescence. Many parents are very supportive of this process, especially when the doctor or nurse involved is someone the parents know and trust to help them keep their teenage children safe.

If you want to develop a more independent relationship with your doctor, here are some suggestions of things to consider:

> ▸ **Talk to your parents about taking an active role in your health care.** Sit down with your parents and discuss with them your desire to be more proactive with your medical care. Tell them that you would like to take control of more things like making doctors' appointments, calling your doctor with questions, and meeting with your doctor alone. If a parent calls and gives permission ahead of time, most physicians will allow teens to go to appointments by themselves.
> ▸ **Compromise.** If you have some things you would like to keep between you and your doctor, ask your parent(s) if you can meet with the doctor alone for the second part of your appointment—that will give you a chance to discuss your more private and personal concerns with him or her. Ideally, your doctor has made this a routine part of visits with teenagers. If not, many doctors will agree to this situation if you request it.
> ▸ **Don't try to cut mom and dad out completely.** There are benefits to keeping your parents involved in your medical care until you are at least 18 years old. For one, they are interested in making sure you get the best treatment possible. Parents can help you make appointments and drive you to the clinic. And unless you are independently wealthy (which most teens are definitely not), your parents' insurance or finances pay your medical bills. If you get a prescription for a medication, like birth control pills or an antibiotic

for an STD, your parents can help you get the prescription filled. So even though most teenagers younger than age 18 can get contraception and STD-related care—even without parents being involved—it is easier to have parents involved if at all possible.

▸ **If you can't talk with your parents, consider confidential care.** Let's face it—in some situations, teens will simply not talk to their parents about sexual health issues. And overall, it is better that these teens get medical care than avoid it because they can't approach their parents. This is why there are state laws that allow many teenagers to get health care services to prevent pregnancy and diagnose and treat STDs without parents being involved. This is called confidential health care.

There are, however, some limits to confidential care. If doctors or nurses are concerned that a teenager under the age of 18 is in danger, they cannot keep these concerns confidential. In most states, the definition of danger is related to concerns about sexual abuse, physical abuse, and risk of homicide or suicide. Doctors or nurses break confidentiality and get other adults involved for two reasons: First, they want to help teenagers stay safe. Second, by law they cannot keep this type of information confidential. In these unusual situations, often the doctors and nurses will talk with the teenager about why they must get other adults involved and discuss with the teenager the best way to do this.

So *where* can you receive these confidential services? Many *pediatricians* and family doctors will treat teenagers confidentially, so consider approaching your physician to see if he or she will do this. Some high schools offer health clinics to students during school hours. Ask your school nurse if yours is one of them. And you can also visit Planned Parenthood or a public health clinic for advice and/or treatment on sexual health issues. Although these clinics are not always free, they offer cheaper health services for teens.

During your appointment, if you feel the doctor or nurse has not answered your questions to your satisfaction, avoids your questions, or seems uncomfortable, consider looking for a new health care provider who will talk openly and honestly with you about uncomfortable topics such as sex. And realize that health departments and Planned Parenthood health centers employ health care providers who are specially trained to be open with clients and to provide them with the most up-to-date information about prevention, testing, and treatment of pregnancy and STDs.

And keep this in mind: Even if you decide to seek confidential health services, a doctor or nurse may encourage you to talk with one or both of your parents. Many teens who initially receive confidential health care do talk with their parents about issues related to contraception and STDs. Health care professionals like doctors and nurses can give you tips on how to talk with your parents, discuss advantages of this type of communication, and help you talk with your parents when it is important to do so.

WHAT YOU NEED TO KNOW

‣ Many teenagers are struggling with the decision of whether or not to have sex.

‣ Numerous teenagers decide to forgo having sex until they are older and more mature.

‣ If you are contemplating having sex, ask yourself, "Is this the right person? Is this the right situation? Is this the right time in my life for sex? And will sex compromise my values?"

‣ People can show their love for each other in many nonsexual ways, including talking, listening, and spending quality time together.

‣ If you decide against having sex, stick to your decision.

‣ If you decide you are ready for sex, remember that you can change your mind at any time, even right before you have intercourse.

‣ If your boyfriend or girlfriend threatens breaking up with you if you don't give in to having sex, you should end the relationship.

‣ If you and your partner decide together that you are ready for sex, and you do not want to become parents, you should discuss what you will use for contraception, and what you will do if you accidentally become pregnant or contract an STD.

‣ Both you and your partner should go to the doctor before you have sex; if you cannot go beforehand, you should go as soon as possible afterward and continue to go once a year to get tested for STDs—you could have an STD and not know it!

‣ If you are going to have sex, use condoms.

> Your chance of getting STDs goes up each time you have sex with a new partner.
> Ask your doctor for vaccines or shots that will protect you from STDs.
> If you do not want your parents to know about your sexual activity, there are some ways you can keep your medical care confidential.
> You can always call an STD hotline with questions or concerns, such as the National STD hotline: 1-800-227-8922.

2

STDs: What They Are and How to Prevent Them

Whether you've chosen to abstain or to have sex, or you're still mulling it over, it is important that you be informed about the dangers of sexually transmitted diseases (STDs). This chapter will give you a crash course on STDs, including what they are, the different forms they take, their prevalence, and the best ways to protect yourself against them.

WHAT ARE STDS?

A sexually transmitted disease (STD) is an infection passed from one person to another through sexual contact. Sexually transmitted diseases are sometimes referred to as sexually transmitted infections (STIs). STIs and STDs are different terms for the same thing: both refer to infections that are passed through sexual behaviors. Although many teenagers think STDs are rare, the United States has among the highest rates of STDs in the industrialized world. In fact, an estimated 19 million new cases of STDs take place every year in this country. Rates of STDs are particularly high among teenagers and young adults. Women are more vulnerable than men to contracting STDs, and they suffer worse symptoms and complications when they get them, but rates are high among both men and women.

HOW ARE STDS SPREAD?

You can get an STD or pass one to another person by having vaginal, oral, or *anal sex*. Condoms significantly lower your chances of contracting an STD, but they aren't foolproof. The only surefire way to avoid STDs is to abstain from sexual activities.

The reason the probability of passing an STD through sexual contact is far higher than through casual contact, such as shaking hands, hugging, or touching, is that most STDs are transmitted through the mucous membranes of the penis, *vulva* (female genitalia), vagina, and mouth. Mucous membranes are different from skin in that they allow certain bacteria and viruses to get into the body.

Although the mouth is considered a mucous membrane, your chances of spreading or contracting an STD through kissing are slim. You are more likely to become infected with an STD through mouth to genital contact, such as while giving *oral sex*. This is because the mucous membranes of the genitals tend to contain many more of the bacteria and viruses that cause STDs than those of the mouth. Some STDs, however, can be transmitted through kissing or simply through skin-to-skin contact, including herpes and HPV. If you have vaginal or anal sex with someone who has STDs, you have a high chance of getting infected.

It is important to know the following:

1. You are at risk for contracting an STD even if it is your very first sexual encounter.
2. The younger you are when you start having sex, the greater your chances of contracting an STD.
3. The more sexual partners you've had, the greater your likelihood of becoming infected.
4. The more sexual partners your partner has had, the greater your likelihood of becoming infected.
5. Having sex without a condom puts you at a much greater risk of contracting an STD than if you have sex that is protected with a condom.
6. Having anal sex without a condom puts you at an especially high risk of contracting HIV from an infected partner.

CAN STDS BE SILENT?

One of the scariest things about STDs is that they often cause no symptoms. You can have an STD and have no clue that you are infected. Your sexual partner can also be unaware, look and feel completely healthy, and actually carry an STD. There are three very important things to know about silent STDs.

First, silent STDs can still be passed during sex. Some STDs carry an equal chance of being spread no matter if symptoms are present or not.

Second, silent STDs can still be causing very serious health problems. For example, silent chlamydia or gonorrhea infections in a female can cause scarring in the *fallopian tubes,* which can lead to *infertility.* Silent HIV infection in men and women seriously weakens the immune system.

Third, doctors and nurses can test you for silent STDs. If you have an infection, a health care professional can diagnose the infection and make sure you get the best treatment.

WHY WORRY ABOUT STDS?

If you do contract an STD, it will be a pretty big deal. STDs are not always silent, and some can make you quite sick. While each STD causes different health problems, overall they can lead to *pelvic inflammatory disease,* infertility, pregnancy complications, cervical and other kinds of cancers, and liver disease. Some STDs also increase your chances of getting HIV/AIDS, a life-threatening disease of the immune system that puts you at risk for other life-threatening conditions and cancers.

In pregnant women, STDs can cause early labor and uterine infections before and after birth. Babies of mothers with STDs may suffer from low birth weight, pneumonia, blood infection, eye infection, brain damage, blindness, deafness, stillbirth, and other conditions.

DO STDS ONLY COME FROM SEX?

For the most part, STDs only come from sex. There are, however, some important exceptions. Some STDs can also be spread through exchange of infected blood. HIV and Hepatitis B are examples of STDs that can also be passed through blood transfusions, sharing injection needles, sharing tattoo needles, and childbirth. Therefore, certain groups of people, such as hemophiliacs (people with a blood clotting disease who must regularly undergo blood transfusions), doctors, and intravenous drug users, are at a greater risk for contracting some STDs through activities other than sexual contact.

WHAT CAUSES STDS?

Although many people will say STDs are caused by sexual activity, this isn't technically true. Sexual activity causes the *spread* of STDs. The infections are actually caused by bacteria, viruses, parasites, and protozoa. In other words, as their name implies, sexually *transmitted* infections are infections spread through sexual contact, not caused by it.

STDs caused by bacteria, parasites, or protozoa can be treated and cured by a doctor or nurse. STDs caused by bacteria include gonorrhea, chlamydia, and syphilis. *Pubic lice* or *crabs* are caused by parasites, and *trichomoniasis* is caused by protozoa.

STDs caused by viruses can be treated but not cured. Those caused by viruses include hepatitis B, herpes simplex, *human immunodeficiency virus* (HIV), and human papillomavirus (HPV).

STDS: AN OVERVIEW

To help you understand the STDs out there and the frequency with which they occur, here is a brief crash course in the most common STDs. We list these infections alphabetically, and all will be covered in greater detail later in the book:

Bacterial vaginosis. *Bacterial vaginosis* (BV) is a condition in women where the normal balance of bacteria in the vagina becomes disrupted and is replaced with an overgrowth of an abnormal bacterium. BV is common in women who are sexually active. Symptoms of BV include a foul-smelling vaginal discharge, itching, burning, and/or pain.

Chlamydia. Chlamydia is the most common curable STD in the United States. In 2007, 1,108,374 chlamydia infections were reported to the Centers for Disease Control and Prevention (CDC). The rates were highest among adolescent girls 15 to 19 years of age and men 20 to 24 years of age. However, since the infection usually causes no symptoms, this number is definitely on the low side. A national study done in 2001–2002 found that, by 18 years of age, about one in 20 young people in the United States are infected with chlamydia without even knowing it.

Chlamydia is caused by *Chlamydia trachomatis,* which can seriously damage a woman's reproductive organs. Even though chlamydia often causes no symptoms, it may silently lead to irreversible damage. Chlamydia can get into the *uterus* and fallopian tubes and cause pelvic inflammatory disease, or PID. If the infection goes untreated, it can lead to infertility.

When symptoms do occur, chlamydia causes abnormal vaginal discharge and burning during urination in women, and it can cause burning during urination and discharge in infected men.

Crabs. Also known as pubic lice, crabs are parasitic insects similar to head lice, except that they nest in the pubic hair. Crabs are usually spread through sexual activity, but occasionally they can spread through contact with an infected person's towels, clothes, or sheets. There is a common misconception that crabs can be spread by sitting on a toilet seat, but the lice cannot live for long away from a warm human body.

Gonorrhea. Gonorrhea is a common STD caused by *Neisseria gonorrhoeae,* a bacterium that grows and multiplies easily in the warm, moist areas of the reproductive tract, including the *urethra* (urine canal) in males and females and the *cervix,* uterus, and fallopian tubes of females. Sometimes called "the clap," gonorrhea can also grow in the anus, eyes, throat, and mouth. Usually women do not have symptoms, but if they do, symptoms include abnormal bleeding, burning during urination, abnormal discharge, and irritation of the vulva. In men, gonorrhea can cause a yellow-pus discharge from the tip of the penis, irritation and redness of the head of the penis, burning during urination, blood in the urine, and swelling in the glands of the groin. In women, gonorrhea can get into the uterus and fallopian tubes and cause pelvic inflammatory disease, or PID. According to the CDC, more than 700,000 people get gonorrhea each year in the United States, but only about half of those new infections are reported. In 2007 there were 355,991 new cases of gonorrhea reported to the CDC.

Hepatitis B. Hepatitis B virus causes inflammation of the liver and liver disease. A person with Hepatitis B may not experience any symptoms, so it's possible for an infected person to be spreading it to others and not know it. When the Hepatitis B infection causes symptoms, a person may experience abdominal pain, jaundice (yellow skin color), and loss of appetite; some will get sick enough to need hospitalization, and it can cause death. Hepatitis B virus can cause a chronic lifelong infection, which greatly increases the chance of liver cirrhosis (scarring) and liver cancer in adulthood.

Herpes. Genital herpes is an STD caused by the herpes simplex viruses type 1 and type 2; most infections are caused by type 2. Herpes often causes no symptoms, but when it does, the symptoms appear as one or more blisters in the area of the genitals or rectum. When the blisters break open, they leave sores that may take two to four weeks to heal. Another outbreak usually occurs within a few weeks or months, but it is almost always shorter and less severe than the first one. Once it infects someone, the herpes virus stays in his or her system forever, and an outbreak can occur at any time. Over time, the number and severity of outbreaks tends to decrease, however.

Genital herpes is common in the United States; at least 45 million people ages 12 and older—one out of five adolescents and adults—

have the herpes virus. The virus is more common in women (one out of four women have the infection) than men (approximately one out of eight men have been infected). This is probably because male to female transmission is more likely than the other way around.

Human immunodeficiency virus/acquired immunodeficiency syndrome (HIV/AIDS). The human immunodeficiency virus (HIV) is an STD that attacks the immune system. The virus specifically attacks your CD4 cells (or T4 cells), immune cells that fight off illnesses. Once the CD4 cell count falls below 200 per cubic millimeter of blood, and/or an opportunistic infection sets in, HIV becomes acquired immunodeficiency syndrome (AIDS). According to the CDC, an estimated 256,363 Americans were living with an HIV infection but did not have AIDS at the end of 2007, and an estimated 455,636 people were living with AIDS.

Symptoms of acute (or recent) HIV infection will develop in some people within six weeks to three months of infection and include fever, rash, muscle aches, and swollen lymph nodes and glands. Then the HIV infection becomes silent for many months to years. HIV infection can be passed to sex partners even when it is silent. As the infection progresses toward AIDS, people with HIV grow increasingly susceptible to illnesses and infections that don't normally affect healthy people.

Human papillomavirus (HPV). Human papillomavirus (HPV) encompasses a group of more than 100 different types of viruses, more than 30 of which are sexually transmitted. HPV may cause genital warts in both males and females, specifically on the penis, vulva (area outside the vagina), anus, lining of the vagina, cervix, or rectum. Current research suggests that about one-third to one-half of sexually experienced young women 15 to 19 years of age in the United States have HPV infection. We really do not have enough good research to know how common this infection is among young men. Luckily, in most people who contract HPV, the infection causes no symptoms and clears up on its own. But not everyone who gets HPV is lucky. Some types of HPV infection can persist for many years and lead to cervical and other genital cancers.

Syphilis. Often called "The Great Imitator" because its symptoms mimic those of other diseases, syphilis is caused by the bacterium *Treponema pallidum.* Syphilis is transmitted through direct contact with a syphilis sore, which can occur on the lips, mouth, genitals, vagina, rectum, or anus. Although syphilis was much more common in the past, the CDC still reported more than 40,000 cases in the United States in 2007.

Symptoms of the primary stage of syphilis include a sore on the area that came in contact with the infection, be it the vagina, anus, penis, or mouth, and sometimes swelling of the glands in the groin. Symptoms of *secondary syphilis*, which usually sets in a few weeks later, may include headaches, general aches and pains, sickness, loss of appetite, a red rash, sores in the mouth, nose, throat, genitals or in the folds of the skin, and fever. Several years later, tertiary syphilis can attack the nervous system, the heart, and the blood vessels, leading to blindness, paralysis, and insanity.

Trichomoniasis. Trichomoniasis or "trich" is a common STD caused by protozoa. Each year, an estimated 7.4 million new cases of trichomoniasis occur. The infection affects both men and women, but women are more likely to have symptoms. In addition to oral, vaginal, and anal sex, trichomoniasis can also be spread by way of contact with wet towels and clothing if the genital area comes into direct contact with these things.

Symptoms of trichomoniasis usually appear within five to 28 days of infection, but sometimes they take as long as six months to show up. They include a frothy yellow-green or gray vaginal discharge with a bad odor, pain during urination and sexual intercourse, and a red, swollen vulva.

MALE AND FEMALE REPRODUCTIVE ANATOMY

The better you understand the male and female anatomies and how they work, the better you will comprehend STDs and how you can avoid them. So here is a quick overview of the male and female reproductive anatomies and their various parts.

THE MALE REPRODUCTIVE ANATOMY

The male reproductive anatomy allows men to produce the sexual hormones and sperm necessary for reproduction. The main parts of the male reproductive anatomy include the penis, *scrotum*, testes, *vas deferens* and seminal vesicles, *prostate gland*, and urethra.

Penis. The penis is the external male organ used for urination and sex. The penis consists of three main parts: the root, the body, and the glans penis. The root is the section that attaches to the abdominal and pelvic wall. The body of the penis is the middle portion, which consists of three cylindrical areas of soft tissue. When a man gets an erection, the two larger cylinders (called the corpora cavernosa) fill with blood, and the penis grows larger. The third cylinder, called the corpus spongiosum, surrounds the urethra, or tube through which urine passes out of the body. Finally, the glans penis is the head of the penis and an extension of the corpus spongiosum. A small ridge called the corona separates the glans penis from the body of the penis.

Scrotum. The scrotum is the thin sac comprised of skin and muscle that contains the testicles. The scrotum holds the testicles slightly away from the body, which keeps them cooler than the normal body temperature and allows for optimal sperm production. Depending on the surrounding temperature, muscles called the cremasteric muscles move the testicles closer to and farther away from the body.

Testes/Testicles. The *testes* are two oval-shaped organs that produce sperm (the male sex cell) and testosterone (the male sex hormone). Their size depends on where an adolescent boy is in puberty. Sperm develop in the testes; tubes attached to the testes called the *epididymis* and vas deferentia transport them.

Vas deferens and seminal vesicles. Once the testicles produce sperm, those sperm travel through a collection area called the epididymis. They then move on to a tube duct called the vas deferens, which joins the seminal vesicles to form what's called the ejaculatory duct. The seminal vesicles, which are located behind the prostate and the bladder, produce a fluid that lubricates the urethra and provides nutrients for the sperm. This fluid, together with other fluids, makes up semen. When a man ejaculates, the muscles surrounding his seminal vesicles contract to push out semen, which contains the sperm.

Prostate gland. The prostate is a walnut-sized gland that surrounds the urethra and lies just below the bladder. Together with the seminal vesicles, the prostate produces a fluid that protects and nourishes the sperm, called the prostatic fluid. This fluid makes up most of the volume of semen.

Urethra. In men, the urethra has two purposes: it transports urine from the bladder to the outside of the body, and it transports semen out the tip of the penis.

THE FEMALE REPRODUCTIVE ANATOMY

The female reproductive system allows women to produce eggs, have sexual intercourse, protect and nourish a fertilized egg while it develops into a fetus, and deliver a baby. Unlike the male reproductive anatomy, the female reproductive anatomy exists almost completely inside the pelvis. It consists of the vulva, vagina, *mons pubis, labia, clitoris,* urethra, *hymen,* uterus, cervix, fallopian tubes, and *ovaries.*

Vulva. The vulva, which means "covering," is the external part of the female reproductive anatomy. Located between the legs, the vulva covers the vagina and other internal reproductive organs.

Vagina. The vagina is a hollow, muscular tube that extends from the uterus to the vaginal opening. In a grown woman, the vagina is about three to five inches long. The vagina serves three main purposes: it is where the penis is inserted during sexual intercourse, it is the pathway for a baby during childbirth (also called the birth canal), and it is the route menstrual blood takes out of the body during a woman's menstrual period. Its muscular walls allow the vagina to hold something as small as a tampon and accommodate something as large as a baby.

Mons pubis. The mons pubis is the fleshy area located just above the top of the opening of the vagina.

Labia. The labia, which means "lips," are the two pairs of skin flaps that surround the vaginal opening.

Clitoris. The clitoris is a small sensitive organ located toward the front of the vulva, where the folds of the labia meet.

Urethra. Located between the clitoris and the opening to the vagina is the urethra, a tube that transports urine from the bladder to the outside of the body.

Hymen. The hymen is a thin sheet of tissue that partially covers the opening of the vagina. There are several activities that can stretch the hymen, including inserting a tampon, vigorous exercise, and sexual activity. Many women experience a torn hymen during their first sexual experience. Although the hymen may bleed when it tears, the amount of pain or discomfort seems to vary.

Uterus. Also called the womb, the uterus is a pear-shaped organ with thick, muscular walls that can expand to accommodate a growing fetus and contract to push a baby out during labor. The uterus contains some of the strongest muscles in the female body. When a woman isn't pregnant, the uterus is about three inches long and two inches wide.

Cervix. The cervix, which means "neck," is the place where the vagina meets the uterus. The cervix has thick, strong walls, and its opening is very small, which keeps things such as tampons out of the uterus. During labor, however, the cervix can expand to allow a baby to pass out of the uterus and through the vagina.

Fallopian tubes. The fallopian tubes come out of the two upper corners of the uterus to connect the uterus to the ovaries. Each fallopian tube is about four inches long and approximately as wide as a piece of spaghetti. The passageway within each tube is even narrower, about the size of a sewing needle. A fringed area that looks like a funnel lies at the end of each fallopian tube and wraps around each of the two ovaries without attaching to them. When an egg pops out of one of the ovaries, it enters the fallopian tube at this fringed opening and travels through the tube toward the uterus with the help of tiny hairs called cilia to push it along.

Ovaries. The ovaries are two almond-shaped organs about 1.5 to two inches in size that sit to the upper right and left of the uterus. The purpose of the ovaries is to produce, store, and release a woman's eggs into her fallopian tubes through a process called ovulation. In addition to producing eggs, the ovaries also secrete the female sex hormones estrogen and progesterone.

HOW CAN STDS BE PREVENTED?

As you will hear over and over again throughout this book, the only way to completely prevent STDs is to abstain from the sexual activities that can transmit them. If you have sex, the fewer sexual partners you have, the less likely you will be to contract an STD. You will also be less likely to contract an STD if you use a condom correctly every time you have sex. Some STDs can be prevented with vaccinations.

Male condoms. Beyond abstinence, the best way to prevent an STD is to use male condoms—they are the most reliable way to decrease risk of contracting an STD. However, condoms are not foolproof. In order for condoms to be most effective, you must use them properly. Plus, the condom can only cover so much. If you or a partner has open herpes sores on an area above the genitals, for example, you could still pass or contract the infection. And there is always the chance that a condom will break, sending all your plans for safe sex out the window. That's why you should think about and prepare for all the consequences of sex—even protected sex—before you decide to engage in any sexual acts.

To properly purchase and use male condoms, do the following:

> ➤ Talk about condoms with your partner before using them.
> ➤ If you think you might have sexual intercourse, keep condoms on hand.
> ➤ Only use latex condoms. If you are allergic to latex, use polyurethane condoms. Condoms made of lambskin and other substances do not protect against STDs. And keep in mind that condoms with *spermicide* are no more effective than spermicide-free condoms at preventing STDs, especially if they contain the popular spermicide nonoxynol-9. In fact, the FDA has advised against using condoms that contain the spermicide nonoxynol-9 because it can increase vaginal irritation, making infection *more* likely.
> ➤ Look for condoms that have a reservoir tip at the end; this leaves room for the ejaculate.
> ➤ Check the expiration date on condoms before you buy or use them; if they are expired, throw them away.
> ➤ Store condoms in a cool, dry place.
> ➤ Do not store condoms in an area where they could become punctured, such as in a desk drawer.
> ➤ Open the condom once the penis has become fully erect and before the penis touches the mouth, vagina, or anus.
> ➤ Squeeze the reservoir tip or top of the condom and unroll it carefully and completely down the shaft of the penis. If it won't roll, it is inside out. Throw it away and use another condom if you have one, because you may have gotten pre-cum or a drop of early ejaculation fluid on it (pre-cum can contain sperm, viruses, and bacteria). If you do not have a second condom, turn it over and roll it on.
> ➤ Make sure the condom fits. If it is too loose, it may not provide a sufficient barrier.
> ➤ Leave about three-fourths of an inch at the tip of the condom for the ejaculate. If you put the condom on too tightly, it can break.
> ➤ Do not use oil-based lubricants or anything else oil-based with condoms—oil can make holes in them.
> ➤ If you feel the condom slip or break during intercourse, pull out and replace it with a new one.

> Be careful not to spill the condom when removing it after intercourse, whether it contains ejaculate or not. HOLD THE RIM OF THE CONDOM when you pull the penis out so nothing spills.
> Do not reuse condoms.
> For oral sex performed on a female, purchase non-lubricated condoms that you split and use flat over the area, or *dental dams*.

The female condom. The *female condom,* a thin sheath or pouch worn by a woman during sex, was approved by the U.S. Food and Drug Administration (FDA) in 1993. It lines the vagina to help prevent pregnancy and STDs. Currently, the FC and FC2 female condoms are the only ones available in the United States.

At this point, not too many women are using the female condom, particularly teenagers. However, information on the female condom can still be valuable, just in case you decide you want to use it.

The FC female condom is a polyurethane sheath pouch about 6.5 inches long with a flexible ring at each end. The ring at the closed end of the condom is inserted in the vagina to hold it in place. At the other end of the condom—the open end—the ring hangs outside the body at the entrance to the vagina. Although the female condom contains some lubricant, it is not a spermicidal lubricant. A new version of the FC female condom, the FC2, became available in 2007; it is the same design as the first version, but it is made of nitrile, which is cheaper to produce.

To use the female condom:

> Open the package carefully.
> Choose a position that is comfortable for insertion—you can sit, squat, lie down, or raise one leg.
> Make sure the inner ring is at the closed end of the sheath and hold it with the open end down.
> Squeeze the inner ring with your thumb and middle finger so it becomes long and narrow and insert the inner ring and sheath into the vaginal opening.
> Gently insert the inner ring into the vagina, place your index finger into the condom, and push the inner ring up as far as it will go. Make sure the condom is inserted straight and isn't twisted inside the vagina.
> Be sure the outer ring is on the outside of the vagina.
> Use enough lubricant so the condom stays in place during sex.

- Guide the penis into the condom to make sure it doesn't slip into the vagina outside the condom.
- Do not use a male condom at the same time as a female condom—the friction may cause one or both condoms to break.
- If the condom slips during intercourse, or if it enters the vagina completely, stop having intercourse and take the condom out. Then insert a new one, adding extra lubricant to the opening of the sheath or to the penis.
- To remove the female condom, twist the outer ring gently and pull the condom out, keeping the semen inside of the condom. Do not put the condom in the toilet; instead, wrap it in the package or some tissue and throw it away.
- Do not reuse the female condom.
- It's best not to use the female condom for anal sex; use a male condom instead.

STD vaccines. There are certain vaccines that can help protect you against STDs. The two vaccines currently available help protect against HPV and hepatitis B infections. After having these vaccinations, you are still susceptible to all of the other types of STDs, so these vaccines should not be used in lieu of abstinence or condoms.

The HPV vaccine. The HPV vaccine currently available protects against four types of HPV, which together cause 70 percent of cervical cancer and 90 percent of genital warts. The FDA recently approved the HPV vaccine for girls and women ages nine to 26. The vaccine consists of three shots given over six months, and it has been tested in over 11,000 women and found to be both safe and effective. The most common side effect is soreness in the area of the injection.

Ideally, girls should get the HPV vaccine before they become sexually active. Women who are currently sexually active also benefit from the vaccine, but they will get less benefit if they have already contracted one of the four types of HPV covered by it. They will, however, get protection for the remaining types.

Experts do not currently know whether or not the HPV vaccine is effective in boys or men. Studies are currently underway to find out.

If you are interested in getting the HPV vaccine—which is a good idea if you are sexually active or planning to become sexually active in the future—talk to your health care professional. Many insurance plans cover the vaccine. In 2008 it cost $120 for a single shot or $360 for the full series, but it may become cheaper over time.

Hepatitis B vaccine. The *hepatitis B vaccine* effectively prevents infection by the hepatitis B virus, a risk factor for liver cancer; therefore, the vaccine has been called "the first anti-cancer vaccine." Studies show the hepatitis B vaccine is safe for children, teenagers, and adults. This vaccine is now recommended for all babies, to give them lifelong protection from hepatitis B infection. If you are sexually active or are planning to become sexually active in the future, talk to your health care professional to be sure you have received the entire hepatitis B series. This is now a three-shot series. If you are late getting one or more shots, you will not have to restart the whole series.

WHAT YOU NEED TO KNOW

▸ An STD is an infection passed from one person to another through sexual contact.

▸ You are at risk for contracting an STD whether you have had many sexual encounters or if it is your first.

▸ The United States has the highest rate of STDs in the industrialized world.

▸ One of the scariest things about STDs is that they often cause no symptoms, so you can be completely unaware that you have one.

▸ While sexual activity causes the spread of STDs, the actually cause of the infections themselves are bacteria, viruses, parasites, and protozoa.

▸ Aside from abstinence, condoms and limiting number of partners are the best ways to prevent STDs.

▸ In order to be effective, male and female condoms must be stored and used properly.

▸ There are currently two vaccines available for the prevention of STDs: the HPV vaccine and the hepatitis B vaccine.

3

Chlamydia

Chlamydia—the most common curable STD in the United States and a leading cause of infertility—is a real threat to teenagers. Chlamydia occurs most often in teenagers and young adults and is a particularly tough problem for teen girls. According to the Centers for Disease Control and Prevention (CDC), in 2007, more than 1 million cases of chlamydia were reported; however, experts know that relying on reported cases underestimates the true number of people infected. Based on the U.S. National Health and Nutrition Examination Survey, nearly 2.3 million Americans between the ages of 14 and 39 are infected with chlamydia. And a study released by the CDC at the 2008 National STD Prevention conference in Chicago revealed that 26 percent (about one in four) of teenage girls between the ages of 14 and 19 are infected with at least one of the most common STDs: chlamydia, human papillomavirus (HPV), herpes simplex virus (HSV), or trichomoniasis.

Chlamydia often causes no symptoms. Because so many people with chlamydia are unaware of their infections, the disease frequently goes undiagnosed and unreported. But if left untreated, chlamydia can have dire consequences, including pelvic inflammatory disease (PID), and scarring that can prevent females from becoming pregnant later in life.

Unfortunately, rates of chlamydia are on the rise. From 1988 to 2007, the number of reported cases of chlamydia in the United States rose from 87.1 to 370.2 cases per 100,000 persons. Although part of this increase has been related to more testing and better tests, it is clear that we now have an STD epidemic—of which chlamydia is a large part. This has become so serious, in fact, that CDC researchers at the 2008 National STD Prevention Conference in Chicago recommended that preventing STDs become an important public health goal.

CHLAMYDIA 101

Chlamydia is caused by the *Chlamydia trachomatis* organism. Chlamydia is a "silent" disease because more than 95 percent of women and men experience no symptoms with the infection. When symptoms of chlamydia do appear, they typically show up within a few weeks after becoming infected.

Chlamydia is often confused with another STD—gonorrhea—and people can have both infections at the same time. Although chlamydia and gonorrhea have similar symptoms (burning with urination, unusual discharge, and bleeding in between menstrual periods) and complications (PID, ectopic pregnancy, and infertility), the two STDs are distinctly different diseases with different treatments.

If chlamydia is caught in time, it can be cured with antibiotics before it causes serious problems. However, if chlamydia goes undiagnosed—which is likely, considering the infection so often produces no symptoms—or if it isn't treated properly, serious complications can arise. In women, untreated chlamydia can spread to the reproductive organs and cause pelvic inflammatory disease (PID), which can lead to permanent damage and infertility. And although complications in men are rare, the infection has the potential to spread and can cause infertility in them as well.

Chlamydia also poses a threat to babies of pregnant women with the infection. Half to 75 percent of babies born to women with chlamydia contract it themselves, and of those, 30 to 40 percent develop complications such as pneumonia or conjunctivitis (pink eye).

Risk factors for chlamydia include being sexually active; engaging in unprotected vaginal, anal, or oral sex; having more than one sex partner; and having a sex partner who has had many partners.

Anyone who has unprotected sex with a partner who has chlamydia can contract this infection; however, certain groups of people are at an increased risk. According to a national health survey conducted by the CDC that looked at more than 6,600 people aged 14 to 39, men and women had similar rates of chlamydia. However, for women, infection was most common in girls ages 14 to 19; and in men, it was most common from age 20 to 29. The infection was also more common in blacks than whites—6.4 percent of blacks versus 1.5 percent of whites. Chlamydia also occurred more often in people who were socioeconomically disadvantaged.

HOW CHLAMYDIA SPREADS

If you are sexually active, you are at risk for contracting chlamydia. Chlamydia spreads during vaginal, anal, and oral sex. Because chlamydia spreads almost exclusively through sexual contact, the more sexual partners you have, the greater your risk for infection. And since chlamydia spreads through oral and anal sex, you are also at increased risk if you are a young man who has sex with men. Even though your chances are increased when you have more than one partner, some people who have only one partner get infected; it just takes exposure to one person with chlamydia to get infected.

In addition, once a teenager has an infection that is treated, many become *re*infected with chlamydia by having sex with an infected partner who has not been treated. Reinfection is extremely common in teenagers; it's so common, in fact, that the CDC recommends repeat testing three to six months after an initial infection and treatment just to make sure reinfection hasn't occurred.

SYMPTOMS OF CHLAMYDIA

In most cases, chlamydia produces no symptoms. When symptoms do occur, they usually show up within one to three weeks after exposure. In women, the chlamydia bacteria first infect the cervix (opening of the uterus) and urethra (urine canal). In many cases, the cervixes of teenage girls and young women have not fully matured, so they are more susceptible to infection.

If you have chlamydia, you may experience unusual vaginal discharge, burning with urination, pain during sexual intercourse, pain in the lower abdomen, and irregular menstrual bleeding. In some cases, chlamydia can also cause a mild fever, muscle aches, or headache. Note that some of these symptoms mimic those of other conditions, such as an allergy, *yeast infection,* or friction from clothing, so some women may dismiss them and neglect to go to the doctor for a diagnosis.

If chlamydia goes untreated, there is a good chance it will spread from the cervix to the fallopian tubes (tubes that carry eggs from the ovaries to the uterus). At this point, some women will still continue to have no symptoms. Others will begin to experience lower

---

Symptom Chart

In most cases, chlamydia produces no symptoms. When symptoms do occur, they may include the following:

Women
- ▶ Unusual vaginal discharge
- ▶ Burning with urination
- ▶ Pain during sexual intercourse
- ▶ Pain in the lower abdomen
- ▶ Irregular menstrual bleeding
- ▶ Mild fever
- ▶ Muscle aches
- ▶ Headache

Men
- ▶ Burning with urination
- ▶ Discharge from the penis
- ▶ Burning and itching around the opening of the penis
- ▶ Pain and swelling in the testes
- ▶ Mild fever
- ▶ Muscle aches
- ▶ Headache

abdominal and back pain, nausea, fever, pain during intercourse, or bleeding in between periods.

When men experience symptoms of chlamydia, they may include burning with urination, discharge from the penis, and burning and itching around the opening of the penis. In rare cases, some men may also have pain and swelling in the testicles.

If chlamydia has infected the rectum (either as a result of transmission through anal intercourse or a genital infection that spread to the rectum), symptoms may include rectal pain, discharge, or bleeding.

DIAGNOSIS OF CHLAMYDIA

If you suspect you may have been infected with chlamydia because you have one or more risk factors for the infection or you are having symptoms, go see your pediatrician, family doctor, adolescent doctor, or *gynecologist.* He or she will probably be able to test you for chlamydia with a simple urine test. You probably won't have to go through a pelvic exam if you are female or a swab in the penis if you are male. There are some doctors' offices that still use pelvic exams and swabs to get a sample from the cervix or penis, however, so ask your doctor which test he or she uses. You can also go to a family planning clinic such as Planned Parenthood, to your local health department, or to an emergency room to be tested.

No matter where you decide to go, make sure you clearly ask for a chlamydia test. Don't assume that your doctor will "read your mind" or "read between the lines" and automatically test you. And remember: a Pap test will not screen for chlamydia and other STDs, so you have to ask for the tests specifically.

While you're at your appointment, you will want to get as much information from your doctor as possible; asking him or her the following questions will help you get the most from your visit:

> ▸ Could I have chlamydia?
> ▸ What treatments are available for chlamydia?
> ▸ What should I tell my partner(s)?
> ▸ What are the symptoms of PID?
> ▸ Could I be infected with other STDs as well?
> ▸ Should I come back for a follow-up?
> ▸ How can I lower my risk of STDs?

If you test positive for chlamydia, be sure that you are also tested for other STDs including gonorrhea, syphilis, and HIV.

CHLAMYDIA TREATMENT

There are specific antibiotics that treat chlamydia. There is no other way of being cured. You have to go see a doctor or nurse and get a prescription medication. If you and your doctor catch the infection in time, antibiotics will eradicate the bacteria in about seven to 10 days. Doxycycline (twice a day for one week) and azithromycin (single dose) are the most common treatments.

If you are taking antibiotics for a chlamydia infection, follow your doctor's orders and finish all of the medication, even if your symptoms go away. And be sure to avoid all sexual activities during treatment, because you can still transmit chlamydia to a partner until the end of your treatment. If your symptoms do not go away within one to two weeks after you've finished your medication, revisit your doctor.

If you are diagnosed with chlamydia, it is crucial that your partner get treated and that any other person you have had sex with in the past 60 days be tested and treated right away, too. Otherwise, he or she could pass the infection right back to you. If it has been more than 60 days since you last engaged in any sexual activity, you should inform your last sexual partner of your infection.

If you are embarrassed about talking with your sexual partner(s) about your chlamydia infection, tell your doctor or nurse. He or she may be able to provide you with information that can help you communicate this difficult news, or you may be able to get something you can send to your partner(s) through the mail in order to avoid a face-to-face conversation.

In addition, doctors in some states now offer *expedited partner therapy* (EPT). With EPT, doctors give a patient antibiotics or a prescription for antibiotics to give to all their sexual partners in attempt to stop the spread of chlamydia. EPT is illegal in some states, however, so ask your doctor about whether or not it is an option for you.

Three to six months after you complete chlamydia treatment, see your doctor. He or she will give you another test to make sure the infection is gone from your body. A follow-up visit is especially important if your sex partner was not treated or if you have a new sex partner.

If you develop PID as a result of untreated chlamydia, you will need two weeks of antibiotic treatment. Your doctor may first prescribe an antibiotic that you can take by mouth or injection. You may also need to stay in the hospital if you cannot take the antibiotics by mouth, are really sick, might need surgery, the antibiotics aren't working, or you are pregnant. You should be retested for chlamydia two to four weeks after you finish antibiotics for PID. PID is a very serious infection, so it is really important to make sure the infection is cured and that you have not become reinfected from a new partner or a partner who was not treated.

POTENTIAL COMPLICATIONS OF CHLAMYDIA

If left untreated or not treated properly, chlamydia can spread to the rest of the reproductive organs. In females, this includes the uterus, fallopian tubes, and ovaries, which can lead to the following:

Pelvic inflammatory disease (PID). Eventually, chlamydia may lead to pelvic inflammatory disease (PID) and infertility. PID is so serious because it can cause permanent damage to the fallopian tubes, uterus, and surrounding tissues. This damage can lead to the following:

▶ Chronic pelvic pain: Ongoing pain in the pelvis, usually due to scar tissue.
▶ Ectopic or tubal pregnancy: A pregnancy that involves a fertilized egg that starts developing in the fallopian tube instead of moving to the uterus. This is a dangerous condition that can be deadly to women.
▶ Infertility: The inability to get pregnant. PID causes infertility by scarring the fallopian tubes, which prevents eggs from being fertilized. The risk of infertility goes up each time you get PID, so if you get PID once, it is really important that you avoid getting it again.

In addition to PID, untreated chlamydia can lead to the following:

Infection of the epididymis. In males, untreated chlamydia can spread to and cause infection in the tubes next to the testicles that store sperm, called the epididymis.

Infection of the urethra. Chlamydia can cause an infection in the tube that carries urine in males and females—called the urethra.

Prostatitis. Chlamydia can spread to the prostate gland in males and lead to *prostatitis*, which causes pain during or after sex, painful urination, lower back pain, fever, and chills.

Proctitis. In people who have anal sex with a chlamydia-infected partner, the bacteria can lead to an infection of the lining of the rectum—called *proctitis*—that causes rectal pain and a mucus discharge.

Infertility in males. In rare cases, untreated chlamydia can cause some men to become infertile.

Increased risk of HIV. For both sexes, chlamydia increases the chances of contracting other STDs, including HIV.

Infections in newborns. Women can spread chlamydia onto their newborns and cause serious infections. Half to three-fourths of babies born to mothers with chlamydia pick up the infection, and 30 to 40 percent develop complications, such as conjunctivitis (pink eye) or pneumonia. Exposed babies can also develop infections in the genital tract, throat, or rectum, and there is some evidence that chlamydia can cause premature birth.

Eye infections. Chlamydia can lead to an eye infection if you touch your eye with a hand that contains the chlamydia bacteria.

Throat infection. The bacteria that cause chlamydia can infect the throat through oral sex.

Reiter's syndrome. In rare cases, untreated chlamydia can lead to a condition called reactive arthritis or *Reiter's syndrome.* Symptoms of this syndrome include knee, toe, or ankle swelling; genital sores; burning during urination; and burning, redness, and/or blurred vision in the eye. Reiter's syndrome is more common in men, but it can also occur in women. Treatment for the condition may include steroid injections in inflamed joints, non steroidal antiinflammatory drugs such as ibuprofen, and painkillers.

Perihepatitis. Females with chlamydia can occasionally develop inflammation around the liver. This is called *perihepatitis,* or the Fitz-Hugh-Curtis syndrome.

PREVENTING CHLAMYDIA

You've heard it before, but the best way to prevent chlamydia in your teenage years is to abstain from oral, anal, and vaginal sex.

Beyond abstinence, the following activities will help reduce your risk of chlamydia.

Be faithful. Stay in a long-term mutually monogamous relationship with a partner who has been tested for chlamydia and determined to be infection-free.

Use condoms. Use latex condoms consistently and correctly every time you have anal, vaginal, or oral sex (for oral sex on a female, use a dental dam). For information on how to use latex condoms, see Chapter 2, page 27.

Use only water-based lubricants. Oil-based lubricants such as vegetable shortening and petroleum jelly will destroy condoms and make them ineffective. Avoid using the spermicide nonoxynol-9. As of December 2007, the U.S. Food and Drug Administration (FDA) issued a new warning for over-the-counter contraceptives that contain spermicide nonoxynol-9. The warning states that vaginal contraceptives containing nonoxynol-9 do not protect against HIV or other STDs. The warning also states that nonoxynol-9 may irritate the vagina and *increase* the possibility of transmitting HIV and other STDs.

Recognize that the only birth control method that helps prevent chlamydia is the condom. Condoms are only effective when used consistently and correctly, and even then, they do not provide 100 percent protection. Other birth control methods, such as the pill, shots, implants, and diaphragms, offer no STD protection.

Communicate with your health care professional. Talk frankly with your doctor or nurse about your sexual history and any STDs you may be at risk for. Don't be embarrassed—doctors deal with this kind of thing every day, and being honest could save your fertility or your life.

Get tested. The CDC recommends a yearly chlamydia test for all women age 25 or younger who have ever had sex, as well as for women older than 25 with risk factors for chlamydia (those with a new sex partner, multiple sexual partners, or who have unprotected sex in a relationship that is not mutually monogamous). Remember that chlamydia often has no symptoms, so you should not wait for signs and symptoms to get tested. If you have ever had sex, go get tested once a year no matter what. Some experts also suggest that all sexually active men ages 25 and younger should be tested for chlamydia once a year, even if they have no symptoms.

If you experience any symptoms of chlamydia, stop all sexual activity and see your doctor. Any unusual genital symptoms, such as abnormal discharge, burning with urination, or bleeding in between menstrual periods, could indicate a chlamydia infection. Early diagnosis will help prevent PID and other complications.

Follow up. If you become infected with chlamydia and are treated for the infection, make sure you see your doctor three to six months following your treatment for another chlamydia test. This will assure that you were not reinfected by the same or new partners.

Partner treatment. If you are infected, your partner(s) need to be treated and cured before you have sex with them again—or you will catch the infection again.

Do not douche. Douching decreases the number of good bacteria in the vagina, which may increase risk of infection with chlamydia and other STDs.

Talk about prevention. Communicate openly with your sex partner(s) about their STD status and your desire to use condoms and/or dental dams.

WHAT YOU NEED TO KNOW

- ▶ Chlamydia is the most common bacterial STD in the United States and a leading cause of infertility.
- ▶ Chlamydia is often referred to as a "silent" disease because over 95 percent of women and men who are infected experience no symptoms.
- ▶ Chlamydia spreads through vaginal, oral, and anal sex.
- ▶ Chlamydia spreads so rampantly in part because it often produces no symptoms. Your sexual partner may think (and therefore claim) he or she is STD-free because he or she has none of the classic symptoms (such as itching and burning during urination) when actually he or she is infected.

- Chlamydia can be passed between partners even when no one has symptoms.
- When chlamydia symptoms do occur, in women they include unusual vaginal discharge, burning with urination, pain during sexual intercourse, and bleeding between menstrual periods. In men, chlamydia symptoms include burning with urination and discharge from the penis.
- Chlamydia is particularly common in teenage girls; a study released by the CDC at the 2008 National STD Prevention conference in Chicago revealed that 26 percent (about one in four) teenage girls between the ages of 14 and 19 are infected with at least one of the most common STDs: chlamydia, human papilloma virus (HPV), herpes simplex virus (HSV), or trichomoniasis. This may at least in part be because the cervixes of teenage girls and young women have not fully matured, so they are more susceptible to chlamydia infection.
- If you suspect you may have been infected with chlamydia, see your doctor. He or she can test you to see if you are infected. This can often be done with a simple urine test.
- If chlamydia is caught in time, it can be completely cured with antibiotics.
- If you are diagnosed with chlamydia, tell anyone you had sex with in the past 60 days that they too need to be tested and treated. If it has been more than 60 days since you had sex, tell your last partner about your infection.
- If you test positive for chlamydia, be sure that you are tested for other STDs as well, including gonorrhea, syphilis, and HIV.
- If chlamydia goes untreated, it can lead to serious conditions, including pelvic inflammatory disease (PID), which can cause ectopic pregnancy and infertility in women. Chlamydia also increases a person's chances of contracting other STDs, including HIV.
- Chlamydia reinfection is extremely common, especially among teenagers. To avoid reinfection with chlamydia, abstain from sexual intercourse until you and your partners have completed treatment.
- Regular testing for chlamydia will help decrease your chances of experiencing complications from the disease if you become infected.
- The CDC currently calls for all sexually active women ages 25 and younger to be tested for chlamydia once a year, even

if they have no symptoms, and for women over age 25 to be screened annually if they have risk factors for the disease.

▶ Some experts suggest that all sexually active men ages 25 and younger should also be tested for chlamydia once a year.

4

Crabs: Pubic Lice

Unless they are at a seafood restaurant or on the beach, most teenagers don't want to be anywhere near crabs—especially the "crabs" that are transmitted sexually. But unfortunately, "crabs," or pubic lice, infect millions of Americans each year, and they are a threat to any teenager who is sexually active. Therefore, it is important that you understand how you can get crabs, how you treat them, and most importantly, what you can do to avoid becoming host to them in the first place.

CRABS 101

Pubic lice are tiny, flat-bodied parasitic insects—one of three types of wingless insects known as lice—that can live on the genital areas of humans. The official name for pubic lice is *Pediculosis pubis,* not to be confused with *Pediculus humanus capitis* (head lice) or *Pediculosis corporis* (body lice). They are similar to the lice you get in the hair on your head, except that they lay eggs in your pubic hair instead. They may also attach themselves to hair on the legs, armpits, mustache, beard, eyebrows, or eyelashes. Pubic lice got the nickname "crabs" because of their crab-like appearance. The good news about crabs is that they aren't dangerous. They are, however, uncomfortable.

Pubic lice live by sucking blood from their hosts, and they get that blood by inserting their mouthpieces into small blood vessels in the skin. Most people experience an allergic reaction to these bites—specifically to the saliva of the pubic lice—which causes intense itching in the pubic region.

In most cases, crabs spread through sexual contact. Rarely, a person will develop crabs after exposure to an infested person's bed linens, towels, or clothes. Symptoms of crabs include itching in the genital area, visible lice eggs (called *nits*), or crawling lice.

There are three stages in the life of a pubic louse—the nit, the *nymph,* and the adult.

Nits. Nits are lice eggs. They are slightly bigger than the period at the end of this sentence, and they are oval and yellowish white in color. If you have pubic lice, you will notice these nits attached to your pubic hair. After the pubic lice lay nits, the nits usually take about a week to hatch.

Nymphs. After six to 10 days, nits will hatch into baby pubic lice called nymphs. These nymphs look very similar to adult pubic lice, except they are smaller. To survive, nymphs suck on the blood from skin in your pubic region. About seven days after hatching, nymphs mature into adult lice.

Adults. Adult pubic lice are about two to three millimeters long, tan or grayish white in color, and they look like miniature crabs when viewed through a magnifying glass. When adult lice fill with blood from their hosts, they may turn a reddish-brown color, making them look like little scabs to the naked eye. Pubic lice have six legs, and the two front ones are significantly larger than the other four and shaped like the pincher claws of a crab. Female pubic lice are slightly larger than the males, and they lay the nits. Like their nymphs, adult crabs feed on human blood to live. If a louse falls off of a person, it will die within one to two days.

HOW CRABS SPREAD

Crabs spread primarily through sexual contact with an infested person; the pubic lice literally crawl from the pubic hair of one person to the pubic hair of the other. They do not fly, jump, or use animals as transportation. Therefore, if you have sexual intercourse with someone who has crabs, chances are good that you will contract them yourself.

You should also keep in mind that because of the nature of pubic lice, you do not have to have sexual intercourse with the person who is infested to pick them up yourself. Pubic lice actually spread quite easily. Any activity that puts your pubic hair in direct contact with someone else's will put you at risk.

One of the reasons pubic lice spread so readily is that they reproduce daily. The female louse survives for an average of 25 to 30 days, and each female lays about three eggs a day, up to a total of 20 to 30 eggs over her three- to four-week lifetime. Pubic lice can also live away from the body for one to two days, so they can hide out in clothing or bedsheets, ready to latch on to the next person's pubic hair.

A common misconception is that you can catch crabs from a public restroom. Although technically it is possible to catch a louse from a toilet seat, pubic lice do not have feet designed to hold onto smooth surfaces like toilet seats; instead, they are designed to attach to coarse body hair, like pubic hair. Therefore, they simply fall into the water and drown rather than hang around waiting for a new host. So the chances of catching crabs from a toilet seat are very rare. Pubic lice also cannot jump from person to person like fleas, and you cannot contract them from animals.

SYMPTOMS OF CRABS

The most obvious symptom of crabs is intense itching in the pubic and/or anal region. In many cases, the itching is worst at night, because the lice become more active then and bury their heads inside pubic hair follicles in order to feed on their host's blood. In addition to itching, pubic lice can cause the following symptoms:

> ➤ Visible lice eggs, or nits, in pubic hair. These nits look like tiny oval yellowish-white dots about the size of a pinhead. They are attached to the hair shaft and are kind of hard to pull off.
> ➤ Tiny tan, grayish, or reddish insects crawling in your pubic hair.
> ➤ More severe skin reactions, such as pustules, in the areas where the pubic lice have been feeding.
> ➤ Bluish-gray marks on your thighs and pubic area caused by bites from the lice.

The pubic lice—and therefore, the itchiness they cause—may also spread to other moist areas of your body as the lice move there, such as your armpits.

Once you've been exposed to pubic lice, it can take up to two to three weeks for the adult lice to show up.

DIAGNOSIS OF CRABS

If you suspect you have crabs, see your doctor—either your pediatrician or family physician or gynecologist—as soon as possible. The longer you wait for a diagnosis, the worse your symptoms will get, and the greater your chances of spreading the infestation on to others. If you'd rather not see one of your doctors for a diagnosis, you can go to a health department clinic, a local sexual health clinic such as Planned Parenthood, or if you are a student, you may have a school health center available. Regardless of where you decide to go, a professional diagnosis is in order. The itching caused by crabs can mimic other conditions, so you will want to make sure you indeed have pubic lice before you start to self-treat.

At your appointment, the doctor will first talk to you about your symptoms and your sexual history. In order to get a proper diagnosis, you should be completely honest about both.

Your doctor will then look closely through your pubic hair for nits, nymphs, or adults, and possibly take some samples and examine them under a microscope. In many cases, it is difficult to spot nymphs and adults because there are very few of them, and they quickly move away from light. If your doctor finds nits, he or she will diagnose you with pubic lice and provide you with treatment.

TREATMENT OF CRABS

In order to get rid of a pubic lice infestation, both the lice themselves and their eggs must be killed. Luckily, lotions and shampoos that kill pubic lice and their eggs are available both with a prescription and over-the-counter at your drugstore. If your doctor confirms that you indeed have pubic lice, he or she will discuss how to get rid of the lice using medication in a drug class called pediculicides, meaning they kill lice. There are several creams or lotions that may be used. Some require a prescription, and some you can purchase without a prescription. Make sure your doctor tells you exactly where you should place the cream and how long you should keep it on. Some creams should be left on for four minutes, some 10 minutes, and others should be left on for eight to 12 hours and then washed off. Make sure you understand what you are supposed to do. Ask your doctor to clarify if it is not clear.

Lindane is a potentially toxic medication, and therefore, it is usually prescribed only after other medications have failed. Lindane isn't recommended for women who are pregnant or breast-feeding. Ivermectin is a pill that is a new option for some people with pubic lice. It is not currently recommended for pregnant or breast-feeding women.

To use prescription or over-the-counter (OTC) lotion, shampoo, or mousse, follow these steps carefully:

1. Wash your pubic area thoroughly and towel dry. The area should also be cool.

2. Read the instructions on the package and follow them carefully. Saturate your pubic hair with the lice medication. If you are using OTC permethrin or pyrethrin, leave the medication on for 10 minutes.
3. Make sure to avoid the mucous membranes at the tip of the penis and the opening of the vagina.
4. Thoroughly rinse off the medication with water.
5. Even after treatment, many nits will stay attached to your pubic hair shafts. To remove them, use a fine-tooth nit comb (usually provided with the medication), tweezers, or your fingernails. If you do not get a nit comb with the medication, you can find one in most drugstores or online. A popular nit comb is the LiceMeister, sold by the National Pediculosis Association.
6. After you have completed the treatment, put on clean underwear and clothing.
7. Machine wash any clothing, towels, or bedding that may have been exposed to the pubic lice on your body or the body of an infested person using the hot water cycle (130° to 160° F). If you're not sure of the temperature of the hot cycle of your home washing machine, take your clothing and linens to a commercial laundromat. Then dry the clothing or bedding for at least 20 minutes on the hottest dryer setting.
8. If you wore any non-washable clothing during your infestation, have it dry cleaned.
9. Inform any people you had sexual contact with while you were infested that they are at risk for infestation themselves. These people should also see a doctor for diagnosis and/or treatment.
10. Abstain from having sex or any form of sexual contact until your treatment is complete.
11. Do not have sex with any partners who may have pubic lice until they have been treated and cured.
12. If you find additional lice or nits after nine to 10 days, repeat treatment.

If your pubic lice infestation has spread to your eyelashes or eyebrows, you should not use the products mentioned above, because they are too harsh. If you only find a few nits or lice in your eyelashes or brows, you may be able to remove them with your fingernails or a nit comb. In the event that you cannot get rid of the nits and/or lice by hand, or if they come back, see your doctor. He or she will be able to prescribe a prescription ophthalmic-grade (safe for the eyes) petrolatum ointment that you can apply to your eyelids two to four times a day for 10 days. (Although Vaseline is also a petrolatum, you shouldn't use it to attempt to get rid of pubic lice on your eyelashes or eyebrows because it can irritate your eyes.)

While you're waiting for treatment to kick in, do your best not to scratch the infected area, because scratching can actually help the lice spread. You can use an antihistamine such as diphenhydramine (Benadryl) to help control the itching. Some people prefer to trim their pubic hair.

Some crab infestations are more stubborn than others. If you still experience symptoms seven to 10 days after your treatment, you may have to re-treat to kill any pubic lice you didn't get the first time. If they persist, definitely see your doctor. Some lice have become resistant, or are no longer killed by the most commonly used medication. In this situation, you will need to be treated with one or more other drugs to get rid of the infection.

Also keep in mind that because pubic lice can live off of the body in clothing and linens—and because they can spread so easily from one person to another—reinfection is common. To avoid reinfection, follow the above treatment steps very carefully and abstain from any sexual contact until you are sure your crabs infestation has been completely cleared—from both your body, your partner's body, and your home. In addition, make sure you re-treat yourself if you continue to spot nits in your pubic hair after your initial treatment. Because they eventually will hatch into nymphs, you need to get rid of all nits in order to be completely cured.

POTENTIAL COMPLICATIONS OF CRABS

Overall, compared with other STDs, crabs are fairly harmless. If they go untreated, however, the little critters can cause some problems beyond simply being an unpleasant annoyance.

The most common complication that results from crabs is incessant scratching, which can lead to worn and broken skin and eventually a bacterial infection if the area becomes extremely irritated and raw. In some cases, relentless itching results from a reaction to the proteins in the saliva of the pubic lice, which get into the skin when the lice bite. If you have been scratching your pubic area a lot as a result of a crab infection, watch for redness or pus—these signs may indicate an infection. If you experience any of these symptoms, notify your doctor right away.

You should also keep in mind that people who have a pubic lice infestation may also have another sexually transmitted infection—an

STD that could be dangerous; so if you have crabs, you should be tested for other STDs as well. And the same goes for your partners.

PREVENTING CRABS

The most effective way to avoid a crab infestation is to abstain from having sexual intercourse or engaging in any type of sexual activity that will put your pubic area in contact with someone else's. Beyond abstinence, here are some things you can do to reduce your risk of getting crabs:

Stay faithful. You can reduce your chances of contracting crabs by staying in a mutually monogamous relationship with someone you know is crab-free. Sexual contact with more than one partner significantly increases your risk of contracting any STD, pubic lice included.

Use condoms. Keep in mind that because they don't cover pubic hair, condoms are not a particularly effective protection against pubic lice. However, whether you are in a mutually monogamous relationship or not, you should use condoms correctly and consistently every time you have sex in attempt to prevent *all* STDs. Just because condoms won't necessarily protect you from crabs certainly doesn't mean you shouldn't use them.

Avoid contact with an infected person. If you know that a sexual partner has pubic lice, you should avoid any intimate contact with that person. This means you should abstain from any and all sexual contact, avoid wearing the person's clothes, refrain from sharing towels, and avoid sleeping in the person's bed.

WHAT YOU NEED TO KNOW

- ▸ Pubic lice, or "crabs," are tiny parasitic insects found in pubic hair. They live by sucking the blood of their hosts.
- ▸ Pubic lice infect millions of Americans each year, and they are a threat to any teenager who is sexually active.
- ▸ Pubic lice spread through sexual intercourse or any sexual contact that puts one person's pubic hair in contact with another person's pubic hair.
- ▸ In some cases, pubic lice live on body hair other than pubic hair, including hair on the legs and armpits, as well as on mustaches, beards, eyebrows, and eyelashes.

➤ Crabs can also spread through contact with an infected person's bedsheets, towels, or clothing.

➤ Unfortunately, because they do not cover the pubic hair, condoms do not protect against pubic lice.

➤ There are three stages of pubic lice—nits (eggs), nymphs (babies), and adults.

➤ The most common symptoms of crabs are intense itching in the pubic region and visible nits or adult lice on the pubic hair.

➤ If you think you have been infected with crabs, see your doctor right away. The sooner you get treated, the sooner your symptoms will subside and the fewer people you will risk infecting.

➤ If your doctor confirms that you indeed have pubic lice, he or she will prescribe a specially medicated shampoo or lotion, or instruct you to find an appropriate product over the counter at your drugstore.

➤ In addition to treating yourself, you will have to wash your towels, bed linens, and clothing in water that is at least 130 degrees Fahrenheit and dry the items for at least 20 minutes in a hot dryer cycle. If you don't have the appropriate laundry facilities at home, take these items to a Laundromat.

➤ Once you have been diagnosed with crabs, it is your responsibility to inform anyone you have sex with of your infestation so these individuals can also be treated.

➤ If your symptoms do not clear up in nine to 10 days after treatment, you may have to re-treat.

➤ Reinfection with pubic lice is quite common, and not all lice are killed by the first medication that you try. If you cannot get rid of lice, or they keep coming back, definitely go talk with a doctor or nurse.

➤ If you have pubic lice, you should go to a doctor or clinic to be tested for other STDs, such as chlamydia, gonorrhea, syphilis, and HIV.

5

Gonorrhea

The sexually transmitted disease (STD) once referred to as "the clap" in the 1960s and '70s seems to be making a comeback. Gonorrhea reached epidemic proportions 40 years ago, but after a national control program was issued in 1975, rates declined. For the past decade, gonorrhea rates have plateaued, and in some states gonorrhea rates have begun to rise. In 2007, 355,991 cases of gonorrhea were reported in the United States. Gonorrhea is now one of the most common bacterial STDs in the country; in terms of reported STDs, gonorrhea is second only to chlamydia. Currently, an estimated 700,000 new gonorrhea infections occur each year. And since gonorrhea occurs most often in teenagers and young adults—the highest rates of infection take place in females ages 15 to 19 and males ages 20 to 24—it is an STD you should be particularly concerned about.

GONORRHEA 101

Gonorrhea is caused by the *Neisseria gonorrhoeae* bacteria. These bacteria grow and multiply easily in warm, moist areas—the cervix (opening of the womb), uterus (womb), fallopian tubes (tubes that transport the egg from the ovary to the uterus), urethra (the tube that carries urine from the bladder to the outside of the body), throat, eyes, and anus. Gonorrhea spreads through vaginal, oral, or anal sex. Therefore, if you are sexually active—particularly if you started having sex before age 18 and you have had multiple sexual partners—you are at risk for contracting the infection.

51

In many cases, gonorrhea produces no symptoms; therefore, many young people are infected with the bacteria but don't know it. Symptoms are much less likely to show up in females than in males, and many females who do have symptoms experience symptoms so vague that they dismiss them for something other than an STD.

When it's caught in time, gonorrhea is completely curable; if left untreated for too long, however, the infection can lead to serious complications, including infertility and pregnancy-related problems. Specifically, untreated gonorrhea may turn into pelvic inflammatory disease (PID), an infection involving the uterus, fallopian tubes, or ovaries in women that can lead to chronic pelvic pain, infertility, and other permanent problems. That's why early diagnosis and treatment is so important.

As mentioned above, gonorrhea rates have overall been stable for the past 10 years, with recent increases seen in a few states. In 2007, the rate of reported gonorrhea in the United States was 118.9 cases per 100,000 people. Any sexually active person is at risk for gonorrhea if he or she has unprotected sex with an infected partner, but the groups with the highest rates of infection are sexually active adolescents, young adults, and African Americans. In fact, from 2003 to 2007 there was a 4.8 percent increase in rates of gonorrhea among people 15 to 19 years old.

HOW GONORRHEA SPREADS

Similarly to most STDs, gonorrhea spreads primarily through sexual activities. You cannot catch gonorrhea from shaking hands, a towel, doorknob, or a toilet seat. You can contract the infection via vaginal, oral, or anal sex or touching one's eye after touching an infected penis or vagina. A mother can pass the infection on to her newborn during childbirth.

SYMPTOMS OF GONORRHEA

Like chlamydia and other STDs, gonorrhea is "silent," meaning it often produces no symptoms, particularly in women. When they do occur, symptoms may be so mild that the person with the infection either doesn't notice them or dismisses them as something else, such as a yeast infection, bladder infection, or friction from clothing. Some females don't discover they have gonorrhea until their male sexual partners contract the infection and begin to exhibit symptoms.

In females, gonorrhea may lead to the following:

- Burning with urination
- Increased frequency of urination
- A yellow-green vaginal discharge that is sometimes cloudy or bloody
- Lower abdominal pain
- Painful sexual intercourse
- Bleeding between menstrual periods
- Heavy bleeding with periods
- Painful lumps from infection of the glands surrounding the genitals

In males, gonorrhea is much more likely to show symptoms—90 percent of males show some symptoms. In males, the infection may lead to:

- Burning with urination
- A tingling sensation in the urethra (the tube that carries urine from the bladder to the outside of the body)
- A yellowish-white discharge that oozes from the tip of the penis

In both males and females, gonorrhea can infect the throat, in addition to the genitals, causing redness and soreness. It can also infect the rectum, causing rectal discharge, anal itching, rectal soreness, bleeding from the rectum, and painful bowel movements.

Symptoms usually appear about two to seven days after a person has been exposed to gonorrhea, but they may take as long as 30 days to show up. Females tend to develop symptoms later than males—on average, about 10 days after they have been exposed to the gonorrhea bacteria.

If you are a female and your gonorrhea infection turns into PID, you may not develop symptoms. Like gonorrhea, PID can be "silent." When symptoms of PID do develop, they may include abdominal pain, particularly in the pelvic region; fever; backache; irregular periods; pain during sexual intercourse; and unusual vaginal discharge.

If it goes on too long without treatment, even if you do not have symptoms, PID can lead to scarring in your fallopian tubes, which will make it harder for you to get pregnant in the future. It also leads to a higher risk of having an ectopic pregnancy (when a fertilized egg grows outside the uterus, usually in a fallopian tube). Ectopic pregnancy always results in miscarriage and can be life-threatening for the mother. Your doctor will typically prescribe at least two different antibiotics, which can be given by mouth or injection, for the treatment of PID.

DIAGNOSIS OF GONORRHEA

If you suspect you may have gonorrhea because you think you might have been exposed, you're experiencing symptoms, or you have a sexual partner who has been diagnosed with the infection, see your doctor as soon as possible. When it's caught early, gonorrhea can be easily cured with the correct antibiotic.

Like other STDs, the symptoms of gonorrhea may seem to subside even though the infection is still raging in your body, so don't take weakening symptoms as a sign that your infection is going away, or that it no longer warrants a trip to the doctor.

If you are uncomfortable seeing your regular physician for a gonorrhea diagnosis, you can go to a local health department or a family planning clinic, such as Planned Parenthood, for a gonorrhea test.

No matter where you decide to go, make sure you clearly ask for a gonorrhea test. Don't assume that your doctor will "read your mind" or "read between the lines" and automatically test you. And remember: a routine Pap test will *not* screen for gonorrhea and other STDs, so you have to ask for the STD tests specifically.

During your appointment, your doctor will test you for gonorrhea by giving you a simple urine test or by swabbing your vagina or penis for discharge. In some cases, the doctor may use more than one test to confirm a gonorrhea diagnosis. The three main tests used for detecting gonorrhea are the following:

> ▸ Gram stain. Your doctor collects a specimen from the cervix or penis with a swab and places it on a slide. The specimen is then stained with a dye and examined under a microscope. This test works better in males than females.
> ▸ Culture. The doctor takes a culture specimen from the cervix or penis and this is monitored in a laboratory for at least 48 hours to look for the presence of gonorrhea. Depending on your symptoms, your doctor may also culture specimens from your rectum, eye, or throat.
> ▸ DNA tests. Also called nucleic acid amplification tests (NAATs), DNA tests examine a specimen from the cervix, penis, or urine for DNA materials from the gonorrhea bacteria. If your doctor orders an NAAT, you will have your results back faster than you will with a culture—usually in 24 hours or less. Your doctor may also be able to perform a DNA test using urine only, sparing you from having to have a pelvic exam if you are a female or a penis swab if you are a male.

Talk to your doctor about which gonorrhea test is best for you. You should also ask to be tested for other STDs at the same time. Teenagers often have gonorrhea and chlamydia infections at the same time, so it's a good idea to be tested for both while you are at the doctor's office.

If you test positive for gonorrhea, be sure you are also tested for other STDs including chlamydia, syphilis, and HIV.

At your appointment, take advantage of the time with your physician to ask him or her any questions you have. You may want to write your questions down ahead of time so you're prepared. Here are some sample questions:

> ▶ Could I be infected with chlamydia as well?
> ▶ If I am infected, what exactly should I tell my partner(s)?
> ▶ How long should I abstain from sex after I start treatment?
> ▶ How do I know if the infection has turned into PID or damaged my reproductive tract?
> ▶ Do I need to be retested after treatment? If so, when should I come back?
> ▶ How can I avoid STDs in the future?

TREATMENT OF GONORRHEA

If your test reveals that you are indeed infected with gonorrhea, your doctor will prescribe antibiotics to kill the bacteria. Luckily, when the infection is caught in time, antibiotics will completely cure it before you experience complications. Gonorrhea infections are now being treated with cephalosporin antibiotics. The Centers for Disease Control and Prevention no longer recommends fluoroquinolone antibiotics because they don't kill some strains of the gonorrhea bacterium. Because strains of gonorrhea have become resistant to certain antibiotics, tell your doctor if you still have symptoms after you finish your medication. He or she will prescribe a different type of antibiotic to better target your individual gonorrhea infection.

Because many people with gonorrhea also have chlamydia, your doctor may test you for both infections. If the doctor does not test you for both infections, he or she may treat you for both with a combination of antibiotics.

During your treatment for gonorrhea, be sure to abstain from all sexual contact to avoid spreading the infection to someone else or becoming reinfected from your partner. You should also finish all of the antibiotics your doctor prescribed for you, even if you start to feel better.

In addition to being treated yourself, you should inform anyone you have had sex with in the past 60 days of your infection and that they need to be tested and treated as well. If it has been more than 60 days since you last engaged in sexual activity, inform your last sexual partner. If you have sex with an infected partner before he or she has been treated, you will get the infection again.

It may be uncomfortable for you to tell past or present sex partners that you have gonorrhea, but it is your responsibility. First of all, you will help the person(s) get quickly tested and treated him or herself, which will reduce his or her chances of complications. And second, if you are still in a sexual relationship with that person, you will protect yourself from being reinfected with gonorrhea. If you cannot talk to a partner directly, consider writing him or her a note or letter, having the doctor write a note that you can give to your partner(s), or bringing your partner with you to a clinic appointment and asking your doctor or nurse to help. In some states, your doctor may be able to write prescriptions for antibiotics that you can give to your partners, which they can use for treatment.

Three to six months after your gonorrhea treatment, see your doctor for another test. This follow-up gonorrhea test will ensure that you have not become reinfected. Having gonorrhea once will not protect you from getting the infection again. In fact, reinfection with gonorrhea is extremely common, particularly among teens. That's why it's so important for your partners to be tested and treated as well—once you have your infection cured, you do not want to catch it again!

If you develop PID as a result of a gonorrhea infection, your doctor will probably prescribe oral antibiotics and give you an antibiotic via injection. Start taking these antibiotics immediately, because the longer you have the infection, the more likely it will be to cause long-term damage, such as infertility or an increased risk of ectopic pregnancy. Also, be sure to take all of the medication you are prescribed. Do not stop the medication just because you feel better. You need to take the full course of antibiotics to make sure all of the bacteria are dead.

In many cases, hospitalization for PID is not required; however, you may need to spend some time in the hospital if you do not respond to the antibiotics, you become severely ill, you are pregnant, or if you develop an abscess (pocket of pus) in your fallopian tubes.

POTENTIAL COMPLICATIONS OF GONORRHEA

When caught early, gonorrhea is easily curable. If left untreated, however, it can lead to serious complications. In females, the infection may continue to produce symptoms such as irregular bleeding and

Symptom Chart

Gonorrhea is a "silent" infection, meaning it often produces no symptoms, particularly in females. When symptoms do occur, they usually show up between two and 30 days after infection and may include the following:

Females

> - An unusual yellow-green, cloudy, or bloody vaginal discharge
> - Lower abdominal pain
> - Burning with urination
> - Increased frequency of urination
> - Painful sexual intercourse
> - Bleeding in between menstrual periods
> - Heavy bleeding with periods
> - A painful lump from infection of the glands surrounding the vagina

Males

> - A tingling sensation in the urethra (the tube that carries urine from the bladder to the outside of the body)
> - Burning with urination
> - A yellowish-white discharge that oozes from the tip of the penis

If gonorrhea spreads to the rectum (which is possible in both males and females):

> - Rectal itching
> - Rectal discharge
> - Bleeding from the rectum
> - Rectal soreness
> - Painful bowel movements

unusual vaginal discharge. Eventually, the bacteria may move to the uterus, fallopian tubes, and ovaries and cause PID, which can lead to scarring and infertility.

Some estimate that about 40 percent of women with untreated gonorrhea will develop PID, so the risk is significant. Of those women, an estimated 20 percent will become infertile, and others may experience life-threatening ectopic pregnancy or pelvic pain on and off for the rest of their lives. The risk of these complications gets higher the more times you have a gonorrhea infection. So, if you have one gonorrhea infection, it is really important that you get treated and cured, and that you never catch gonorrhea again.

In pregnancy, gonorrhea can spread to a newborn during birth and cause problems for the baby, including meningitis (an inflam-

"Mutual Monogamy" and STDs

1. Alison and Bob feel strongly about monogamous relationships. They have been together for six months in a mutually monogamous relationship. Do they have to worry about STDs?

   Yes, if either has ever had sex before. If either one has had sex, he or she is at risk for having a silent STD, or an STD that doesn't produce symptoms. Many STDs are silent, so many people bring them to a new relationship without realizing it. So whenever you have sex with a new person, you are being exposed to whatever he or she has been exposed to in the past.

2. Rachel first started having sex two years ago. She has had four serious relationships since then. Each relationship lasted about four months, and during each relationship, she and her partner were loyal and only had sex with each other (mutually monogamous). Rachel did not use condoms because in each relationship she trusted her partners' loyalty.

   Dave first started having sex two years ago. He has not had what he considers serious relationships, but he has had sex with four different casual partners and did not use condoms. Who is at higher risk of STDs?

mation of the membranes that surround the brain and spinal cord), joint infection, a life-threatening blood infection, or a serious eye infection that can lead to blindness. It may also lead to premature delivery. Therefore, all pregnant women should be screened for gonorrhea.

In males, gonorrhea can spread to the epididymis (the tube attached to the testicle that helps transport sperm). There, the infection can cause pain and swelling in the testicles, create scar tissue, and lead to infertility. Gonorrhea can also cause scarring of the urethra, making urination difficult.

In both males and females, gonorrhea may spread to other parts of the body, including the skin, joints, throat, eyes, heart, brain, and the area around the liver.

Rachel and Dave are BOTH at high risk. They have each had four different partners in their lifetime and not used condoms. They have each exposed themselves to any STD their four partners may have brought to the relationship.

3. Beth has only had sex with one person her whole life. She and her partner use condoms during the time of the month she thinks she might get pregnant, but not during the times of the month when she thinks her risk of pregnancy is low. Does Beth need to worry about STDs?

It depends on whether her partner has an infection. If her partner has an STD, she is at very high risk of getting infected. Her partner could have a silent infection with gonorrhea, chlamydia, syphilis, HSV, HIV, or any other STDs, and if so, Beth will likely become infected even though she has only had sex with one person. THIS HAPPENS IN REAL LIFE. Furthermore, it is extremely difficult to know for sure when a female can and cannot get pregnant, so despite what she may think, Beth is also at risk of pregnancy.

Beyond the above, gonorrhea can also lead to the following complications.

Increased risk of HIV. Teens with gonorrhea are at an increased risk of acquiring HIV compared to teenagers without the infection. Both gonorrhea and chlamydia seem to raise risk of HIV by stimulating the body to produce more of the white blood cells to which the HIV virus attaches.

Anorectal gonorrhea. If you have anal sex—either homosexual or heterosexual—with someone infected with gonorrhea, you may develop a gonorrhea infection in your rectum. This may cause itching, bleeding, discharge from the anal region, or no symptoms at all. You can also get *anorectal gonorrhea* as a result of a genital infection that has spread to your rectum.

Pharyngeal gonorrhea. If you have oral sex with someone infected with gonorrhea, you may get a gonorrheal infection in your throat, which can cause pain with swallowing and redness of the throat and tonsils.

Eye infection. If the gonorrhea bacteria reach your eye—usually because you touched an infected penis or vagina and then touched your eyes—it can lead to conjunctivitis (pink eye). Conjunctivitis causes a red, inflamed eye and, in rare cases, blindness.

PREVENTING GONORRHEA

No one wants to have a gonorrhea infection. So when it comes to gonorrhea—and all other STDs—prevention is your best bet. Because it is sexually transmitted, the best thing you can do to prevent gonorrhea is to abstain from all types of sexual activities, including vaginal, oral, and anal sex.

Beyond abstinence, the following actions will help prevent gonorrhea:

Limit your number of sexual partners. The more sexual partners you have, the higher your chances of contracting gonorrhea and other STDs.

If you're in a relationship, be faithful. Stay in a mutually monogamous relationship with a person you know has been tested for gonorrhea and determined to be infection-free.

Use condoms. Use a latex condom correctly every time you have vaginal, anal, or oral sex. Condoms are the only birth control method that will prevent gonorrhea and other STDs. For information on how to use a condom properly, see chapter 2, page 27. In most cases, when a condom fails, it is due to human rather than manufacturing errors. Keep in mind that even when used properly, condoms are not 100 percent effective.

Use dental dams for oral sex. If you plan to engage in oral sex on a female, use a dental dam. Dental dams are flat, latex barriers, and they are available in medical supply stores. If you don't have a dental dam, you can also use a condom cut lengthwise or a piece of non-microwavable saran wrap placed over the vagina. Avoid brushing or flossing your teeth right before you have oral sex—both actions may tear the lining of your mouth, making exposure to gonorrhea and other STDs more likely.

Use only water-based lubricants. Do not use oil-based lubricants such as petroleum jelly or vegetable shortening during sex, because these substances may weaken the condom and make it ineffective. If you want to use a spermicide along with a condom, use it according to the manufacturer's instructions. Also watch out for birth control products that contain the spermicide nonoxynol-9. As of December 2007, the U.S. Food and Drug Administration (FDA) mandated a new warning for the labels of over-the-counter vaginal contraceptives that contain nonoxynol-9, stating that the spermicide does not protect against HIV or other STDs. In fact, the FDA warns that nonoxynol-9 can actually increase vaginal irritation, making transmission of HIV and other STDs *more* likely.

Recognize that the only birth control method that helps to prevent gonorrhea is the condom. Condoms are only effective when used consistently and correctly, and even then, they do not provide 100 percent protection. Other birth control devices, such as the pill, shots, implants, and diaphragms, offer no protection.

Get tested regularly. The Centers for Disease Control and Prevention recommend that all young women age 25 and younger get tested for gonorrhea, chlamydia, and some other STDs once a year. Since gonorrhea usually causes symptoms in males, if you don't have symptoms as a male, you won't be tested at a routine exam.

Talk to your doctor. Communicate openly with your doctor or nurse about any STDs you may be at risk for. Don't be embarrassed—doctors deal with this kind of thing every day, and being open and honest could save your fertility or your life. Although doctors may encourage you to talk to your parents, these types of conversations between adolescents and doctors and nurses should be confidential.

Do not douche. Most women who *douche* do this because they think is will make them cleaner. However, douching actually increases the risk of infection with gonorrhea and other STDs because it changes the natural flora of the vagina and may actually flush bacteria higher in the genital tract where it can cause infection. There is no medical reason to douche, and douching can cause problems.

Get tested if you think you're at risk. Gonorrhea often produces no symptoms—particularly in females; so if you think you may have been exposed to gonorrhea, see your doctor immediately for a test.

Young women should be tested once a year. The CDC recommends that once a young woman starts having sex, she should be tested for gonorrhea once a year, even if she feels completely well, until she is 25 years old.

If you have gonorrhea, make sure you do not have other STDs. If you test positive for gonorrhea, be sure you are also tested for other STDs, including chlamydia, syphilis, and HIV.

If you have a positive test, your current sexual partner and/or any partners you have had in the last 60 days should also be tested and treated if infected. If it's been more than 60 days since you last had a sexual encounter, the person you were with last should get a gonorrhea test.

Talk to your partner(s). Communicate openly with your sex partner(s) about their STD status and your desire to use condoms and/or dental dams. You will catch the gonorrhea again if you continue to have sex with an infected person.

WHAT YOU NEED TO KNOW

▶ Gonorrhea is an STD caused by the *Neisseria gonorrhoeae* bacteria, and it is a common sexually transmitted infection in the United States.

- The highest rates of gonorrhea infection occur in women ages 15 to 19 and men ages 20 to 24.
- Gonorrhea can spread through vaginal sex, oral sex, anal sex, or from a pregnant woman to her newborn during childbirth.
- In many cases, gonorrhea produces no symptoms, so many teenagers who are infected do not know it.
- When symptoms do occur, they usually show up between two and 30 days after a person has been exposed to gonorrhea.
- Gonorrhea symptoms are much less likely to show up in females than in males.
- When gonorrhea is caught in time, it is easily curable. So if you suspect you have been infected with it, you should see your doctor as soon as possible for treatment.
- If gonorrhea is left untreated for too long, it can cause serious complications, including pelvic inflammatory disease (PID) in women, an infection that can lead to chronic pelvic pain and infertility.
- In men, untreated gonorrhea can lead to pain and swelling of the testicles, scar tissue in the urethra, and infertility.
- If a pregnant woman passes gonorrhea onto her newborn during childbirth, the bacteria can cause serious problems in the baby, including meningitis and conjunctivitis.
- Teenagers with gonorrhea are at an increased risk of contracting HIV compared with teens who are not infected.
- At your doctor's appointment, make sure you clearly ask for a gonorrhea test; otherwise, your physician may not order one.
- Your doctor may be able to use a DNA test for gonorrhea, which tests urine and will spare you from having to have a pelvic exam if you are a female or a penis swab if you are a male.
- Teenagers often have chlamydia and gonorrhea at the same time, so it's a good idea to be tested for both STDs at once.
- If you test positive for gonorrhea, your doctor will most likely prescribe a cephalosporin antibiotic.
- While you're being treated for gonorrhea, you should abstain from all sexual contact to avoid spreading your infection.
- You should inform anyone you had sex with in the past 60 days of your infection so he or she can also be tested and treated. If it has been more than 60 days since your last sexual encounter, notify the last person you were with.
- If you have sex with your partner before he or she has been cured, you will catch it again.

- Having gonorrhea once will not protect you from future infection; in fact, re-infection with gonorrhea is extremely common among teenagers.
- Abstinence is the best way to prevent gonorrhea.
- Beyond abstinence, you should limit your number of sexual partners, stay in a monogamous relationship with someone you know is gonorrhea-free, use condoms every time you have sex, and use only water-based lubricants.
- Females under age 26 should get tested regularly—at least once a year—for gonorrhea, even if they have no symptoms.

6

Hepatitis

When you think of sexually transmitted diseases (STDs),
hepatitis B probably isn't one of the first infections to come to your
mind. But it should be. Hepatitis B is a serious and potentially fatal
disease caused by a virus, and it can be spread by activities that
some teenagers engage in, such as sex or getting a piercing or tattoo,
or injecting drugs. Hepatitis B infections can lead to serious complications, such as liver scarring (called cirrhosis) and/or liver cancer.

INTRODUCTION TO HEPATITIS

The term *hepatitis* means "inflammation of the liver." Your liver
is the organ located on the right side of your abdomen, just below
your lower ribs. Your liver does many important things to keep you
alive, such as fighting infection, stopping bleeding, filtering poisons
from your blood, producing bile (the greenish fluid stored in your
gallbladder that helps you digest fat), and storing energy. Your liver
also produces cholesterol and certain proteins.

Luckily, your liver is very resilient, and if it gets inflamed it can
regenerate and heal itself by replacing injured tissues and cells with
healthy ones. Yet despite its fighting power, your liver is still vulnerable. When the liver gets inflamed it may not recover, and it could
become permanently damaged. Some people die of hepatitis.

Hepatitis can be caused by a number of things. The liver can
become inflamed when a person drinks too much alcohol. Some

medications also can inflame the liver. In teenagers, however, it is often caused by an infection with the hepatitis virus. Once the hepatitis virus enters the bloodstream, it infects the liver and causes inflammation (hepatitis). Sometimes a person's body can clear the infection on its own. At other times the body cannot clear the infection, and it can remain in the body and cause severe liver damage and, in some cases, death.

There are six different types of hepatitis viruses known today (hepatitis A, B, C, D, E, and G), but you should be most concerned with three of them: hepatitis A, hepatitis B, and hepatitis C (HAV, HBV, and HCV).

Hepatitis A usually spreads through fecal–oral transmission. You can contract it through oral or anal sex, but it is usually transmitted through food or water that has been contaminated by feces. You can prevent hepatitis A with the hepatitis A vaccine.

Hepatitis C usually spreads through the passing of infected blood. It is possible to get it through sexual intercourse, but sex is not a common means of transmission.

Hepatitis B, the form we will focus on in this chapter, is the type of hepatitis that is most directly linked with sexual activity; it can spread from one person to another through blood and other bodily fluids, such as semen and vaginal secretions. You can prevent hepatitis B with the hepatitis B vaccine.

HEPATITIS B 101

Your risk of contracting HBV is real in your teenage years. Each year, more than 4,000 people die from HBV, according to the Centers for Disease Control and Prevention (CDC), and most of the 80,000 Americans who get the infection are teenagers or young adults. An estimated 1.25 million adults in the United States have a chronic HBV infection, 20 to 30 percent of whom acquired the infection when they were children or teenagers.

The good news is that the rate of HBV infection in the United States is declining. According to the CDC, the number of new infections per year dropped from an average of 260,000 in the 1980s to about 60,000 in 2004, and the fastest decline has taken place among children and teenagers, probably due to the HBV vaccine.

As you will learn in this chapter, the ways to prevent infection with HBV include:

1. Getting vaccinated against Hepatitis B (all THREE shots)
2. Abstaining from sex

3. Using condoms consistently and correctly every time you have sex
4. Limiting your number of partners if you have sex
5. Avoiding injection drugs
6. Making sure needles are sterilized if you get piercings or tattoos

ACUTE HEPATITIS B

"Acute" hepatitis B means a person has a new or recently acquired infection. Luckily, as many as 95 percent of teenagers with HBV will develop antibodies and clear the virus out of their bodies on their own. In these teenagers, the virus will last less than six months. Some people with acute HBV infection will not have symptoms, and others will become quite sick.

CHRONIC HEPATITIS B

The remaining 2 to 6 percent of teenagers will not clear the virus and will develop what is known as chronic infection with HBV, an infection that lasts six months or longer. As many as 1.25 million Americans have a chronic HBV infection.

A teenager's chance of developing a chronic infection is lower than that of babies and young children. According to the CDC, chronic HBV infection occurs in 90 percent of infants infected at birth, 30 percent of children infected between the ages of one and five, and six percent of people who are infected after age five. In chronically infected people, chronic liver disease develops in approximately 15 to 25 percent of cases.

If HBV becomes chronic it can be very serious, potentially leading to liver damage and/or liver cancer. And babies born to mothers with HBV have a 90 percent chance of having the infection themselves unless they receive a special immune-strengthening injection and a first dose of the HBV vaccine as soon as they are born.

HOW HBV SPREADS

A person who is infected with the hepatitis B virus can pass it on when their blood or bodily fluids come in contact with another person. More specifically, HBV can spread from one person to another by way of a few activities, including the following:

Having sex with someone who is infected with HBV. If you have unprotected vaginal, anal, or oral sex with someone who has

HBV, you can contract the virus through exposure to infected blood, saliva, or semen. Specifically, during sexual intercourse, the secretions of someone who is infected can enter your body through small tears in your genital area or rectum. You can also become infected with HBV if you use a sexual device that was used by someone else and wasn't washed properly or covered with a condom.

Needles. If you share IV drug paraphernalia with someone who has HBV, you will be at risk for contracting the virus through exposure to infected blood. The best way to prevent HBV is to avoid using needles altogether, but if you do use needles, you should participate in a needle exchange program in your area. These programs allow you to exchange used needles for new sterile ones. In addition, you should seek counseling or treatment for your drug use.

Another way you can contract HBV through needles is by way of an accidental needle stick. Health care providers and other people who work with human blood are at risk for HBV infection through accidental sticks, and therefore, they should be vaccinated against the virus and be extremely careful when handling needles or other sharp instruments.

Passing the virus onto an unborn baby. Pregnant women with HBV can pass the infection on to their unborn babies. If you are pregnant and have HBV, your baby can get a shot of hepatitis B immune globulin at birth, followed up by the first in a series of hepatitis B vaccines to greatly reduce infection.

In addition, you can get HBV through exposure to blood of an infected person through sharing razors, toothbrushes, washcloths; getting a tattoo or body piercing with equipment that isn't sterile; exposure to someone in your home who has a chronic HBV infection; and exposure to an infected person when traveling to countries where HBV infection is common.

Despite some common myths, you cannot get HBV through food or donating blood. You also cannot get HBV from shaking hands, sneezing, hugging, coughing, dancing, sharing a swimming pool, holding hands, or sitting next to an infected person.

SIGNS AND SYMPTOMS OF HEPATITIS B

Hepatitis B causes different symptoms in different people. In many cases, HBV leads to symptoms similar to those of the flu, but many people—an estimated 50 percent—experience no symptoms at all. Signs and symptoms usually don't set in until one to four months after infection (the typical range is 45 to 160 days), and they can range from mild to severe. If you become infected with HBV, you may experience any or all of the following symptoms:

- Yellow tinged skin and eyes (called jaundice)
- Loss of appetite
- Extreme tiredness
- A bloated and sore abdomen
- Nausea and vomiting
- Joint pain
- Fever
- A rash all over your body
- Dark-colored or brownish urine
- Light-colored stools

Even if you experience no symptoms at all, the hepatitis B virus may still be silently damaging your liver, which is why testing for the virus is so important if you suspect you may have been exposed or if you engage in behaviors that put you at risk.

DIAGNOSING HEPATITIS B

If you suspect you may have been exposed to HBV, or if you experience symptoms of the infection, see your doctor as soon as possible. If you were very recently exposed, the doctor may be able to give you treatment to reduce your chance of catching the infection. If you have the infection, the earlier you get a diagnosis the better off you will be.

If you'd rather not make an appointment with your doctor, you can also get tested for HBV at a hospital or public health clinic. In many public health clinics, testing for HBV and other STDs is free.

To test for HBV infection, your doctor will take a sample of your blood. He or she will then run one or more specific blood tests to look for the virus. The results of the blood test will show whether or not you have HBV and if so, how serious the infection is.

Here is a quick breakdown of the specific blood tests your doctor may use:

Hepatitis B surface antigen (HBsAg). The hepatitis B surface antigen is the outer surface of the hepatitis B virus. If you have a

Symptoms Chart

Some people with HBV infection do not develop symptoms. If a person does develop symptoms, HBV infection usually takes an average of one to four months to produce them. When symptoms do set in, they usually include:

➤ Yellow tinged skin and eyes (called jaundice)

➤ Loss of appetite

➤ Fatigue

➤ Abdominal pain

➤ Nausea and vomiting

➤ Joint pain

➤ Fever

➤ A full-body rash

➤ Dark-colored or brownish urine

➤ Light-colored stools

positive HBsAg test, it means you are infected with HBV and can easily pass the infection on to other people.

Antibody to hepatitis B surface antigen (anti-HBs). If you get a positive result from this blood test, it means you have antibodies to HBV in your blood. This may mean you were previously infected with HBV and recovered, or that you have been vaccinated against the infection. Either way, it means you are protected from the virus and cannot infect other people.

Antibody to hepatitis B core antigen (anti-HBc). If you test positive for anti-HBc, it may mean you have a chronic HBV infection and are at risk for infecting other people. However, it also may mean you are currently recovering from an acute HBV infection.

Your doctor may use the results of the other two blood tests to help interpret the meaning of your anti-HBc test. If you get uncertain test results, your doctor may decide to repeat all three tests.

In addition to the above three blood tests, your doctor may decide to order some additional tests to check the severity of HBV infection and the condition of your liver.

POTENTIAL COMPLICATIONS OF HEPATITIS B

As mentioned above, most people who become infected with HBV clear the virus out of their systems on their own. Not everyone is so lucky, however. In some people, HBV lasts longer than six months and eventually leads to severe problems. These problems may include the following:

Serious liver diseases. Because HBV attacks the liver, it may eventually cause liver diseases like cirrhosis and liver cancer. According to the CDC, liver cancer occurs in 15 to 25 percent of people with chronic HBV infections. And if you had HBV as an infant or child, you are at risk for developing liver problems as an adult.

Liver failure. In extreme cases, HBV can cause your liver to shut down completely, a condition called acute liver failure. If this occurs, you will need a liver transplant to stay alive.

Hepatitis D. An HBV infection automatically puts you at an increased risk for another form of hepatitis, hepatitis D (HBD). Once known as the delta virus, HBD uses the outside coat of HBV virus in order to infect cells. In a way, HBV acts like a food for HDV. You can't become infected with HDV unless you already have HBV. If you become infected with both HBV and HDV, you will be even more likely to develop liver failure, cirrhosis, or liver cancer than someone who has HBV alone.

TREATING HEPATITIS B

If you have recently been exposed to the HBV virus, you should see your doctor right away. Your doctor may be able to give you a shot of immune globulin; this contains antibodies against HBV, and it can prevent you from coming down with the disease.

If you have the infection, you can discuss treatment with your doctor. Early treatment will not only make you feel better and help to prevent serious complications, it also will lessen the chances that you will spread the infection to others. You can be monitored by your doctor to make sure a hepatitis infection is going away on its own, or to determine whether it is more likely to become chronic.

If an HBV infection becomes chronic, there are treatments available, but they will not cure the infection completely. You will need to be evaluated by a doctor who is a specialist in liver diseases on a regular basis, and you will need to abstain from drinking alcohol in order to prevent the liver disease from getting worse.

In addition, there are some medications that may help keep HBV under control. These drugs include Adefovir dipivoxil (Hepsera), interferon alfa-2b, pegylated interferon alfa-2a (Pegasys, Intron A) lamivudine (Epivir HB, Baraclude), and telbivudine (Tyzeka).

IF YOU HAVE HBV

If you have HBV, as we discussed above, you need to see a doctor regularly. A healthful diet will increase your energy and keep your immune system strong. If you feel nauseated, try small meals throughout the day and eat foods that are easy to digest, such as soups, broths, or a plain baked potato. If you're having trouble eating, a registered dietitian can help you find foods that are both healthful and appealing.

In addition to eating a healthful diet, you should get enough sleep and exercise regularly (if you feel up to it) to keep your body strong. You should also avoid drinking alcohol and stop taking anything that could be toxic to your liver, including Tylenol.

In some cases, people with HBV become so sick that they cannot eat or drink. If you fall into this category, you may have to be hospitalized until you can keep food and liquids down on your own.

If HBV causes severe liver damage, some people will eventually need a liver transplant. This is a surgical procedure that involves taking out the old, damaged liver and putting in a new healthy one from a donor.

PREVENTING HEPATITIS B

Unfortunately, HBV is a very contagious virus. Researchers estimate that HBV is 100 times more contagious than HIV, even though it is spread in the same ways. Any activity that puts you in direct contact with another person's blood puts you at risk for HBV.

The best way to prevent HBV is with the HBV vaccine. Among teenagers who get the virus, about half deny ever having sex or using drugs, so doctors aren't sure where they got it. That's why *everyone* should get the HBV vaccine.

The HBV vaccine prevents both infection with HBV and the complications that sometimes go along with the virus. According to the National Immunization Program, the HBV vaccine protects 90 percent of adults and 95 percent of children from infection with HBV.

And you can rest assured that the vaccine is safe. The HBV vaccine has been used in the United States since 1982, and the American Academy of Pediatrics, the CDC, and the American Academy of Family Physicians all recommend the HBV vaccine for children and teenagers ages 0 to 18. More than 70 million children and adults have been vaccinated, and more than one billion people have gotten the vaccine worldwide. Over the past 10 years, the HBV vaccine has contributed to the dramatic drop in the number of cases of HBV in teenagers.

The HBV vaccine is given as a series of two or three shots over a six-month period. If you do not get all of the shots in the allotted six months, you do not need to start them over; you can complete the series late. No matter which schedule you have, you will need all shots in the series in order to be protected. Side effects of the vaccine typically include soreness and redness at the site of injection; more serious side effects are very rare.

Vaccination against HBV is recommended for the following groups of people:

- All children and teenagers under the age of 18
- People with multiple sex partners
- People who have been diagnosed with another STD
- Men who have sex with men
- People whose sexual partners have been infected with HBV
- Injection drug users
- People who live in the same home as a chronically infected person
- Infants born to mothers infected with HBV
- Health care and public safety workers
- Patients on hemodialysis
- People with other liver diseases
- Infants born in areas with high rates of HBV infection

If you haven't gotten the HBV vaccine and are interested in getting it, talk to your health care professional. You can get the series of shots right in your doctor's office, and some school clinics and city or county health departments offer the vaccine. For more information on the HBV vaccine, call the CDC-INFO Contact Center at 1-800-232-4636.

In addition to the HBV vaccine, the FDA has approved hepatitis B immune globulin (HBIG) to help prevent HBV in people who have already been exposed. HBIG is particularly effective for preventing HBV in babies who have been exposed to the virus in their mother's wombs.

The second best way to prevent HBV is to avoid the activities that make transmission of the infection likely. HBV spreads easily through blood and other bodily fluids, and you can prevent it by doing the following:

> ▸ Abstain from vaginal, anal, and oral sex. Similarly to other STDs, the best way to prevent HBV is to avoid sexual acts that can expose you to blood, semen, or vaginal secretions.
> ▸ Always use a latex condom when you engage in sexual activities. If you do decide to engage in sexual acts, the best way to help prevent HBV is to use latex condoms correctly every time you have sex. Although condoms are not 100 percent effective in preventing HBV, they will definitely cut down your risk of contracting the infection. For instructions on how to use condoms properly, see Chapter 2, page 27.
> ▸ Use a condom or dental dam during oral sex. To protect yourself from HBV infection during oral sex, use a condom during oral sex on a male or a dental dam during oral sex on a female. If you don't have a dental dam, you can use a piece of saran wrap or a split condom to cover the genital area.
> ▸ Limit your number of sexual partners. Each time you have sex with a new person, you greatly increase your risk of getting any STD, including HBV.
> ▸ Avoid contact with an infected person's blood. You can come in contact with infected blood in a number of ways, most likely through sexual contact or sharing needles.
> ▸ Stay away from intravenous drugs and any shared drug paraphernalia.
> ▸ Take the correct steps if you plan to travel internationally. If you plan to visit a region where infection with HBV is common, talk to your doctor about getting the HBV vaccine well in advance of your trip. This will allow the antibodies to build up in your body, so you will be best protected against infection.

➤ If you travel to a foreign country and receive blood products while you are there for any reason, make sure you get tested for HBV as soon as you get home. Although the blood supply is now well screened in the United States, this is not the case in some other countries. The prevalence of chronic HBV is high in Africa, Southwest Asia, the Middle East, the South and Western Pacific Islands, the interior Amazon River basin, and certain parts of the Caribbean (Haiti and the Dominican Republic).

➤ Avoid sharing toothbrushes, razors, washcloths, or anything else that can transmit blood or other bodily fluids.

➤ Don't get a tattoo. Tattoo and piercing parlors sometimes reuse needles on customers without properly sterilizing them first. If you get a tattoo or piercing, make sure you carefully research the tattoo and piercing places you are considering.

➤ Get tested if you are pregnant. If you know you're infected with HBV during pregnancy, you and your doctor can take the appropriate steps to protect your baby from the virus.

WHAT YOU NEED TO KNOW

➤ Every child and adolescent in the United States should get the HBV vaccine.

➤ If you are exposed to HBV after having taken all of the HBV vaccine shots, your chances of catching the virus are extremely low.

➤ Hepatitis B is a serious and potentially fatal disease caused by the HBV virus, which specifically attacks the liver.

➤ Hepatitis B specifically attacks your liver.

➤ HBV is the form of hepatitis that is most directly linked with sexual activity. It spreads from one person to another through blood and other bodily fluids.

➤ Ninety-five percent of teenagers who get HBV clear the virus out of their systems on their own.

➤ In the remaining five percent, HBV infection becomes chronic, which can lead to cirrhosis or liver cancer.

➤ Abstinence is the most effective way to prevent exposure to HBV.

➤ Beyond abstinence, you should use a condom correctly every time you have sex, avoid sharing needles, and avoid getting a tattoo or piercing, with needles that have been used on another person.

➤ Similar to other STDs, you may have an HBV infection and not have symptoms; the only way to know for sure if you have been infected is to get a blood test(s) from your doctor.

➤ If you could have been exposed to HBV, see a doctor right away.

7

Herpes

For Ellen, age 17, one night changed the rest of her life. After drinking too much at a party, Ellen had unprotected sex with a male friend. About two weeks later, her genital area was covered with painful blisters, a fate that comes back to haunt her a few times each year. Ellen has genital herpes.

Unfortunately, genital herpes is quite common in the United States, teens included. At least 45 million people ages 12 and over—or one in five teenagers and adults—have a genital herpes infection.

Genital herpes is a sexually transmitted disease (STD) caused by a virus, so it cannot be cured. Once you've been infected, herpes lives in your body forever, and it can rear its ugly head at any time.

Although genital herpes usually does not lead to serious health problems, the sores associated with the infection are painful and embarrassing and, as mentioned, there is no cure. If you contract herpes, like Ellen, you will have to deal with the threat of an outbreak of painful sores on your genitals for the rest of your life. That's why prevention is so important.

HERPES 101

The herpes viruses can cause painful sores on the mouth or genitals. There are two types of the herpes virus—herpes simplex 1 (HSV-1) and herpes simplex 2 (HSV-2). HSV-1 is the herpes virus that usually causes sores on the lips, mouth, and gums, called fever blisters or cold sores. HSV-2 is the herpes virus that usually causes genital herpes. However, both HSV-1 and HSV-2 can be spread via contact with someone who is infected during oral, anal, or vaginal sex. This means that HSV-1 and HSV-2 can cause sores on the mouth or the genital area. Both HSV-1 and HSV-2 are incurable and stay with you for life.

Like many other STDs, herpes can be silent, meaning an infected person may not necessarily show symptoms. Even if an infected person has no symptoms, he or she can still pass the herpes virus to others. Therefore, you or someone else with the virus can pass it on to another person without knowing it.

When genital herpes symptoms do occur, they typically take the form of one or more blisters on or around the genitals or rectum. These blisters eventually break, leaving open sores that may take two to four weeks to heal the first time they occur. From that point, the virus stays in the body indefinitely, so an outbreak can reoccur at any time. Usually, another outbreak takes place a few weeks or months after the first, and it is most often less severe. People with genital herpes have several outbreaks per year. Luckily, there are treatments available for herpes that help prevent recurrent outbreaks and minimize their severity, but these treatments do not offer a cure.

Beyond the regular outbreaks the herpes virus causes and the nuisance and embarrassment that go along with them, the virus also leads to other potential complications. For one, over time, the stress of never knowing when an outbreak is going to occur can take its toll emotionally and socially. A genital herpes infection also puts you at a higher risk for contracting the HIV virus and other STDs. Plus, if you or your partner becomes pregnant, you could pass the infection during delivery and cause a potentially fatal infection in your baby.

HOW HERPES IS TRANSMITTED

You can contract genital herpes by having vaginal, anal, or oral sex with someone who has the virus. Experts used to think that people could only spread herpes when the virus was active and producing symptoms, but today they know that is not true. In fact, experts now think that herpes spreads most often when no symptoms are present (this is called "asymptomatic transmission"). In one study that followed couples in which only one person was infected with HSV-2, when the virus was spread from one partner to the other, in 70 percent of cases, it was at a time when the infected partner showed no symptoms.

You can also get genital herpes if your genitals touch the infected skin or secretions (i.e., vaginal secretions, semen, or saliva through oral sex) of someone with a herpes infection; in other words, there doesn't have to be penetration for you to be at risk.

HSV-1 most commonly causes sores on the mouth and lips (fever blisters), but it can also cause sores on the genitals by way of oral-genital contact with a person who has the virus. In fact, HSV-1 causes an estimated 30 percent of genital herpes cases in the United States, most of which are presumed to have spread through oral sex.

DIAGNOSIS

As mentioned, genital herpes doesn't always cause symptoms. Up to two thirds of people with the virus never have symptoms. But when genital herpes does produce symptoms, it often leads to flu-like

Don't Be Fooled

"I can't catch herpes if he's not having an outbreak."
Although health care professionals used to think that the only way to contract genital herpes was to have oral, anal, or vaginal sex with someone who was having an active outbreak, today they know this just isn't true. In fact, in one study of couples in which one partner was infected with genital herpes and the other was not, in 70 percent of cases, the virus spread from the infected to the uninfected partner when no symptoms were present. About 20 percent of the time, or about 72 days a year, genital herpes undergoes a process called shedding, where the virus is active in the urinary and genital tract, but there are no symptoms.

"If I'm only giving or receiving oral sex, herpes isn't a concern."
Although you are less likely to spread or contract the herpes virus by giving or receiving oral sex than you are by having anal or vaginal sex, oral sex is still risky. If you or your partner has genital herpes, it can spread to the other person's mouth. On the flip side, if you or your partner has oral herpes, it can spread to the other partner's genitals. To avoid spreading herpes through oral sex, do not have oral sex when you or your partner is having an outbreak, either orally or genitally. And in between outbreaks, always use a condom during oral sex on a male or a dental dam during oral sex on a female.

symptoms, such as a fever, headache, swollen glands, painful urination, and blisters or sores on or around the vaginal area, on the penis,
around the anus, or on the buttocks or thighs. In some cases, sores
can also appear on areas of the skin that have come in contact with
another sore.

After you have been exposed to the herpes virus, the first sores
(called the "primary" outbreak or episode) usually pop up within a
week or two and heal within two to four weeks. As the sores heal,
scabs may form on skin surfaces, such as the buttocks or penis. Sores
will heal without scabs on mucous membranes, like the vagina.

Once you contract herpes, the virus remains dormant in a bundle
of nerves at the base of your spinal cord forever, causing periodic
outbreaks of blisters a few times a year. Most people with recurrent
genital herpes have about four to five outbreaks a year, each of which
lasts for five to 10 days. There are a few possible triggers for these outbreaks, including stress, infections, and menstruation, but outbreaks
can also occur for no apparent reason. About half of infected people
who have recurrent outbreaks will receive some prewarning of an
outbreak in the form of tingling and irritation in the area of infection
a day or two before it occurs. Luckily, over time, herpes outbreaks
usually become less frequent.

As a side note, other STDs can also cause sores, such as syphilis.
So if you have sores for the first time, see your doctor as soon as possible. If you have a history of herpes outbreaks and you experience
an unusual sore, you should still get checked.

SHOULD I BE TESTED?

You should get checked for genital herpes if you have any symptoms
of the virus, such as an unusual sore or sores, or if you discover that
your partner has genital herpes or has symptoms of the disease.

You can get checked for genital herpes at your pediatrician, gynecologist, or family physician's office, the health department, a community clinic, or Planned Parenthood. Or, you can call the CDC's
National STD and AIDS hotlines at 1-800-227-8922 or 1-800-232-4636
to find low-cost or free clinics in your area.

If you visit your doctor because you suspect infection with the
herpes virus, he or she will probably take a sample from one of your
sores and send it to a laboratory for testing. If you don't have sores at
the time of your appointment, your doctor might give you a blood test
to look for antibodies to HSV-1 or HSV-2 infection. But keep in mind
that, if you have a blood test, your results may not show up positive
until several weeks after exposure to the herpes virus.

Symptoms Chart

Genital herpes doesn't always lead to symptoms, but when it does, it can cause the following:

Primary infection or first outbreak symptoms usually occur about a week or two after initial exposure and produce the following symptoms:

> - Flu-like symptoms, such as fever, headache, achy joints, swollen glands
> - Painful urination
> - Blisters or sores around the vaginal area, on the penis, around the anus, or on the buttocks or thighs
> - Scabs on skin surfaces where the sores initially appeared

Recurrent outbreaks usually occur four to five times a year for about 10 days at a time and produce the following symptoms:

> - Tingling or irritation in the area of infection a day or two before an outbreak occurs
> - Sores or blisters around the vaginal area, on the penis, around the anus, or on the buttocks or thighs
> - Outbreaks that usually become less frequent and severe over time

If your test for genital herpes turns out to be positive, that means anyone you've had vaginal, anal, or oral sex with may also be infected. Be sure to tell your recent partners of your diagnosis so they too can have a test. You should also be tested for other STDs, since you may have acquired another infection when you got genital herpes. And from now on, you should *always* use a latex condom when you have sex. (Remember: You can pass on the infection even when you do not have symptoms). While you have visible sores, avoid all sexual contact.

Genital Herpes Myths

There are a few myths floating around out there about genital herpes that should be dispelled. For one, some people think that the virus lives on public toilet seats, doorknobs, utensils, bedsheets, or hot tubs, but this simply isn't true. Also, in the past, doctors thought that infection with the HSV-1 virus reduced the chances that a person would contract HSV-2; today, experts believe the two viruses are separate and therefore, a person can have both HSV-1 and HSV-2 at the same time.

TREATMENT

There is no cure for genital herpes, but some antiviral medications can help treat the symptoms. The drugs acyclovir (Zovirax), valacyclovir (Valtrex), and famciclovir (Famvir) are all prescription antiviral drugs that help control herpes. If you contract genital herpes, your doctor will help you decide whether taking a medication is best for you.

Medication schedules work by either preventing outbreaks or by helping the sores to heal faster. If you have multiple outbreaks a year, you can reduce your chances of passing the infection onto your sexual partners by taking daily medication, a treatment called daily suppressive therapy. People usually take suppressive therapy if they have six or more genital herpes recurrences a year.

You can also receive treatment for acute genital herpes symptoms, called episodic treatment. As soon as you see or feel signs of an outbreak, you take treatment for seven to 10 days.

Beyond medication, simply knowing you have the herpes virus and must anticipate an outbreak may make you feel worried, sad, or depressed. Feel free to express your emotions with your health care professional; not only will he or she be able to provide treatments to lessen the number and severity of your outbreaks, he or she will also be able to give you tools to handle the emotional burden or refer you to a mental-health professional. In addition, numerous genital herpes support groups throughout the country can provide outlets for you to express your feelings and experiences, as well as provide you with additional information. Remember, genital herpes is common and you are not alone. One such site is the International Herpes Alliance, at http://www.herpesalliance.org. To find a support group in your area, check out the support groups listed by area at the American Social Health Resource Center at http://www.ashastd.org/herpes/herpes_comm_support.cfm.

PREVENTION

As mentioned, because herpes stays in your body indefinitely after infection, the best thing you can do is to prevent infection in the first place. Abstaining from having sex is the most effective way to protect yourself from the virus.

If you have sex, the best way to prevent genital herpes is to have sex with only one person who does not have herpes. Since herpes can be a silent STD, it will be very difficult to know for sure whether your partner is herpes-free. It is important to use a latex condom every time you have sex. If you use them correctly each and every time you have sex, condoms can greatly reduce your chances of getting genital herpes. For information on how to use condoms correctly, see Chapter 2, page 27. But keep in mind that a condom will only protect the area of the body that it covers. If you or your partner has herpes sores or blisters on an area not covered by the condom, you can still spread the infection.

When it comes to oral sex, you should always abstain when one partner is experiencing an outbreak, either on his or her genitals or mouth. Between outbreaks, you should use a dental dam during oral sex. A dental dam offers protection to both partners during oral-vaginal sex on a female or oral-anal sex on a male or female. It is a small, thin, square piece of latex that acts as a barrier between the genitals or anus and mouth secretions during oral sex. To use a dental dam, first rinse off any powder from the latex and then hold it against the vulva or anus of the partner receiving the oral sex. Do not flip the dental dam over and use the other side for another round—this will expose both you and your partner to the bodily fluids you were trying to avoid. Dental dams are available in some medical supply stores. If you don't have one handy, you can use a split and flattened unlubricated condom or a piece of saran wrap.

A large part of preventing herpes is communication. If you plan to have sex with a new partner, you have every right to ask him or her if he or she has genital herpes. As mentioned a few times throughout this chapter, you can contract the virus from someone who is currently symptom-free. And if you yourself have genital herpes, you owe it to your prospective partners and yourself to be honest about the infection. It may be uncomfortable at first, but in general, people infected with genital herpes get used to talking openly about the virus with prospective partners over time.

WHAT YOU NEED TO KNOW

▸ Genital herpes is an STD caused by a virus, so it cannot be cured.

▸ Genital herpes leads to blisters and sores on the genital area, which can be both painful and embarrassing.

▸ There are two kinds of herpes—herpes simplex 1 (HSV-1), and herpes simplex 2 (HSV-2).

▸ In general, HSV-2 causes blisters on the genital area, and HSV-1 causes blisters on the mouth.

▸ Like many other STDs, herpes often causes no symptoms.

▸ Genital herpes can spread whether or not symptoms are present.

▸ Once a person becomes infected with genital herpes, the virus lives in his or her body forever, and an outbreak can take place at any time.

▸ Genital herpes can be transmitted through vaginal, anal, or oral sex.

▸ The only way to avoid genital herpes completely is to abstain from vaginal, anal, and oral sex.

▸ Condoms offer some protection against genital herpes, but they only protect the areas of the body they cover.

▸ You should never have sex with someone while you or the other person is experiencing a herpes outbreak.

8

HIV/AIDS

Of all the STDs, human immunodeficiency virus (HIV) is the most frightening. This is the virus that causes Acquired Immunodeficiency Syndrome (AIDS), which, in most cases, is eventually fatal. Since the AIDS epidemic began, more than 50,000 teenagers have contracted HIV. HIV progresses to AIDS. Many of these teens have died before reaching the age of 20.

According to the CDC, in 2006 there were 19,200 young people between 13 and 29 years of age who found out that they were infected with HIV. This was the highest number of new infections found in any age group. From 2003 through 2007, the estimated number of adolescents who found out they had AIDS increased. From the beginning of the epidemic through 2007, the CDC estimates that 292 adolescents ages 13–14, 1,143 adolescents 15–19, and 8,880 young adults 20–24 have died of AIDS.

There is good news. The total number of new HIV infections is declining due to better awareness of how the disease is spread and measures to prevent infection. In the United States, the number of new HIV infections peaked at 150,000 per year in the mid 1980s and has declined to about 40,000 per year currently. These numbers show that when it comes to HIV, prevention works. However, there is also bad news. The CDC reports that since the late 1990s, the rate of HIV infection among teenagers and young adults has started to rise again. So it is particularly important that teenagers do whatever is in their power to prevent HIV.

WHAT IS HIV?

HIV is the virus that causes AIDS. HIV destroys a type of defense cell in the immune system called the CD4 helper lymphocyte. CD4 lymphocytes play an important role in fighting infectious diseases; specifically, they act as messengers to other types of immune system cells, telling them to become active to fight an invading bacteria or virus; so as HIV destroys these CD4 cells, people get serious infections that they would normally fight off.

Once a person's CD4 cells reach a certain low point, he or she is said to have acquired AIDS. Most people develop AIDS about 10 to 15 years after having been first exposed to the HIV virus. AIDS is a very serious disease that breaks down the body's immune system, its main defense against illnesses. In short, people with AIDS are vulnerable to many different diseases and infections that healthy people are immune to.

HIV/AIDS is so serious because there is no cure. HIV is a virus, and so far, no cures have been found for viruses. Recently, the fate of people who acquire HIV/AIDS has improved, because drugs have been developed that can help keep the disease under control for a longer period of time, but researchers have not been able to find a way to get rid of the virus from the body completely.

The HIV virus spreads by way of sexual fluids (semen from a man or vaginal secretions from a woman) or blood of an infected person. Overall, the infection can be transmitted if an infected person's blood or other bodily fluid comes in contact with blood, mucous membranes, or broken skin of an uninfected person. If HIV-infected blood or sexual fluid enters your body, you are at risk for infection.

The specific acts that carry a risk of contracting or transmitting HIV include vaginal sexual intercourse, anal intercourse, and oral sex. Most teenagers who become infected with HIV are exposed through some sort of sexual act.

There are also some activities that carry no risk of transmitting HIV, including closed mouth or social kissing, hugging, cuddling, or shaking hands with an infected person. It also cannot be transmitted through mosquito bites, sneezes, sharing glasses or water fountains, by touching door handles, or by masturbating.

The CDC has documented only one case of HIV transmission that may have been attributed to contact with blood during an open-mouth kiss. Because open-mouth kissing may be a risk factor, the CDC recommends that you avoid it with a person who is known to be or may be HIV positive.

WHAT IS THE DIFFERENCE BETWEEN HIV AND AIDS?

HIV is the virus that causes AIDS. AIDS is classified as a "syndrome" that breaks down the immune system, leaving the victim vulnerable to a whole host of diseases, including liver disease, pneumonia, and serious infections of the brain and other internal organs. The amount of time between when a person is infected with HIV and when he or she is diagnosed with AIDS depends on a variety of factors. For one, many people don't know exactly when they were infected with HIV, because the initial symptoms of the infection are often vague or nonexistent.

There are many drugs that can delay the progression of HIV to AIDS. Because different people have different responses to these drugs and start taking them at different times during the course of the disease, their effectiveness at delaying the onset of AIDS varies.

SYMPTOMS OF HIV/AIDS

Some people experience symptoms of acute HIV infection two to four weeks after they have been infected that resemble the flu or infectious mononucleosis ("mono"). These symptoms may include:

- Fatigue
- Fever
- Decreased appetite
- Headache
- Swollen lymph glands
- General malaise
- Muscle stiffness or aching
- Rash
- Sore throat
- Ulcers in the mouth or throat

Most people with HIV have no symptoms at all for a long time. Eventually, when HIV weakens the immune system enough, a person develops AIDS. This can take 10 to 15 years. Once HIV has progressed to AIDS, symptoms may include the following:

- Weight loss
- Frequent fevers

> Night sweats
> Extreme fatigue
> Swollen glands in the neck, groin, or armpits
> Persistent skin rashes
> Severe herpes infections
> Short-term memory loss
> Rapid weight loss
> White spots in the mouth or throat
> A cough that won't go away
> Persistent vaginal yeast infections in women

HOW DO TEENAGERS GET HIV/AIDS?

Since the AIDS epidemic surfaced in the early 1980s, many myths and stereotypes have emerged about the disease. Drug users, white gay males, and prostitutes have been labeled as the types of people who get AIDS, but in reality, AIDS does not discriminate based on lifestyle, race, or age. Any human being, from an elderly man in a nursing home to a teenage girl with straight A's to a middle-aged female college professor, can contract HIV/AIDS. As a teenager, you and your friends are just as vulnerable to HIV/AIDS as anyone else.

One of the scariest aspects of HIV/AIDS transmission is that there is no way to tell if a person is infected. People can live for years and years with HIV and appear perfectly healthy. In fact, the Centers for Disease Control and Prevention (CDC) estimates that one quarter of the people infected with HIV in the United States do not know they are infected. The only reliable way to find out if you or someone else has been infected is with an HIV test.

Behaviors that increase the risk of contracting HIV/AIDS include:

Vaginal sexual intercourse. Whether you are male or female, you can contract HIV by having unprotected sex with someone who is infected. Condoms decrease this risk, but they do not eliminate it completely.

Anal sexual intercourse. HIV can also be spread through anal intercourse, either between two men or a man and a woman. Again, condoms lessen this possibility, but they do not take it away. Anal sex is the sexual activity that carries the highest risk of spreading HIV. One group of people particularly vulnerable to contracting HIV through anal sex is men having sex with men (MSM).

Oral sex. Oral sex, when one person kisses, licks, and/or sucks the genital area of another person, carries some risk of HIV infection. For example, if a person sucks the penis of an infected man, he or she can ingest infected fluid through the mucous membranes in his or her mouth. The virus could also enter the body if there are any bleeding gums or tiny sores in the mouth (which can easily be there without a person knowing it). The same thing can happen when someone performs oral sex on a female. Unfortunately, oral sex is too often put in the "totally safe" category when it comes to HIV and other sexually transmitted infections when it shouldn't. Although the risk of contracting HIV via oral sex is lower than through vaginal or anal sex, the risk is still real. Don't falsely believe that oral sex is safe when it comes to preventing HIV and other STDs. If you are going to engage in it, use a male condom or female dental dam for protection.

Using drugs that you inject or snort. If you inject drugs and share needles with someone, you might as well be blood brothers or sisters. Blood from one person gets sucked into the needle and then injected directly into the next person who uses it. Injected drug use is the cause of an estimated 11 percent of HIV infections in people ages 13 to 24. And although it is not addressed nearly as often as the risk of IV drug use, you can also contract HIV if you share straws to snort drugs; blood can be passed from the inside of one person's nose to another via the snorting device.

Tattoos or piercings. You are also at an increased risk of HIV/AIDS if you have gotten tattoos or piercings. Many tattoo parlors are safe and clean, but there are some that are not good about using clean needles and piercing equipment, and it is tough to tell the difference between the two. Therefore, you should recognize the risk that goes along with any tattoo or piercing you choose to get.

HOW CAN TEENAGERS PROTECT THEMSELVES FROM HIV?

The only way you can completely protect yourself against HIV and AIDS is to abstain from having any kind of sexual intercourse, be it vaginal, anal, or oral sex. Not only will abstaining from sex protect you from HIV/AIDS, it will also prevent contraction of other STDs.

Remember: there is no way to tell by looking at a person whether or not he or she has been infected with HIV. The virus can take

Don't Be Fooled:

"HIV really isn't a big deal anymore. You just take drugs for it, and it doesn't really affect you that much."
True, there are powerful medications available today that help fight the HIV virus and therefore keep people with the disease alive longer than ever before. However, these medications are not a cure. Eventually, HIV leads to AIDS, and usually a person with AIDS will die because of it. And in the meantime, side effects of HIV medications are not pleasant—they include diarrhea, fat accumulation in the stomach and neck, extreme fatigue, rashes, and vomiting. Plus, these medications cost thousands of dollars per year, they have to be taken many times each day, and they often lead to kidney and liver disease. In summary, you shouldn't rely on HIV medications to protect you in the event that you become infected; the best way to protect yourself is to remain HIV negative in the first place.

"Only gay people and drug users get AIDS."
HIV/AIDS does not discriminate based on age, sexual orientation, socio-economic status, or lifestyle factors. If you engage in behaviors such as

years to progress to AIDS, so someone can look perfectly healthy and still carry the disease. You also cannot rely on asking someone if he or she is infected because (1) he or she may be infected without knowing it and (2) there are people who will say whatever you want to hear to coerce you to have sex.

The only way for you or someone else to know if they are infected is with an HIV test.

If you do choose to engage in sexual intercourse, use condoms every time. For tips on how to use both male and female condoms properly, refer to page 27 in Chapter 2. A dental dam is a small, thin, square piece of latex that provides a barrier between the genitals or anus and mouth secretions during oral sex. To use the dental dam, first rinse off any powder from the latex and then hold it against the vulva or anus of the partner receiving the oral sex. Do not flip the dental dam over and use the other side for another

IV drug use or unprotected sex, you put yourself at risk for HIV/AIDS, no matter what your age or background. And remember—although having lots of sexual partners will put you at a greater risk, you only have to have had unprotected sex *once* with an infected partner to contract HIV/AIDS.

"Only older people get AIDS—I'm not going to catch it from another teenager."
Wrong again. People ranging in ages from newborn babies to the elderly in nursing homes have HIV/AIDS. According to the CDC, in 2006 there were 19,200 young people between the ages of 13 and 29 who found out they were infected with HIV. This represented the highest number of new infections found in any age group. From 2003 to 2007, the estimated number of adolescents who learned they had AIDS increased. From the beginning of the epidemic through 2007, the CDC estimates that 292 adolescents ages 13–14, 1,143 adolescents ages 15–19, and 8,880 young adults 20–24 have died of AIDS. Teenagers are at risk because adolescence is a time when young people engage in behaviors that put them at risk for contracting HIV, such as drug use and unprotected sex.

round—that will expose both partners to the bodily fluids they were trying to avoid and negate the whole purpose. If you do not have a dental dam, the CDC says you can also use a cut-open condom that makes a square or plastic food wrap.

If you use IV drugs, you should use a clean needle each time you use. If you use drugs that you snort, use a clean straw or other snorting device each time. If you or a friend or loved one has a problem with drugs or alcohol, you can seek professional help through your local doctor or call the National Clearinghouse for Alcohol and Drug Information at (800) 729-6686.

Another thing you can do to reduce your risk of HIV/AIDS is to avoid getting tattoos or piercings. Although many tattoo and piercing parlors are safe and clean, there are some whose practices are less than sanitary; for example, some reuse needles and piercing devices, which can spread HIV through infected blood. To offer yourself maximum protection, skip the piercings and tattoos. Or, at the very least, make sure you carefully research the establishments you visit.

Beyond that, because HIV can be transmitted through blood, if you are going to touch another person or another person is going to touch you (whether it is a sexual situation or you are working in a doctor's office or hospital), make sure any cuts on your skin are covered with bandages or Band-Aids.

GETTING TESTED FOR HIV

Although the thought of finding out you have been infected with HIV may be frightening, you will be much better off if you know. If you have HIV, getting a definitive diagnosis will assure that you get treatment early on, so you can stay healthier longer. It is important that HIV positive people begin treatment as soon as possible to delay the onset of AIDS. Plus, once you know whether or not you are infected, you will be able to take the appropriate steps to prevent passing the disease to your partners or to a baby should you or your partner become pregnant. In addition, getting tested will help you do the socially responsible thing if the test turns out to be positive—inform all your sexual partners so they can get tested too.

As you read this, you may be wondering, "Should I get tested?" That's a good question—it can be tough to figure out whether you are at a significant enough risk for the disease to warrant a test. The Centers for Disease Control and Prevention has recently recommended that all people ages 13 to 64 should be tested for HIV, and that people at a high risk for HIV be retested at least once a year. This means that if you have ever had sex, the CDC now recommends that you have at least one HIV test. You should be tested for HIV every year if you fit into any of the following categories:

> - You have injected drugs or steroids or shared injection equipment (such as needles, syringes, works) with others.
> - You have had unprotected heterosexual or homosexual vaginal, anal, or oral sex with men who have sex with men, multiple partners, or anonymous partners.
> - You have exchanged sex for drugs or money.
> - You have been diagnosed or treated for a sexually transmitted disease, such as syphilis, gonorrhea, or chlamydia, or you've been diagnosed or treated for hepatitis or tuberculosis.

➤ You have had unprotected sex with someone who fits into any of the above categories.

Once you have decided to be tested, there are several places you can go for the actual test. If you want, you can talk to an adult—a parent, school nurse, or trusted relative—about where to go for an HIV test. These are options to consider and discuss:

➤ Family doctor
➤ Pediatrician
➤ Gynecologist
➤ Local health department
➤ Planned Parenthood clinic
➤ AIDS clinic

If you are unsure how to get an HIV test, or you have general questions, you can call the National AIDS Hotlines at (800) 232-4636 (English) or (800) 344-7432 (Spanish) for help.

No matter where you decide to go, you should be tested as soon as possible and then again in six months if you think you may have recently been infected. This is because the virus is difficult to detect immediately after a person has been infected.

When considering an HIV test, one of the things on the minds of many teenagers is, "will I have to tell my parents?!" If you are under 18 years of age, it depends on where you live. Laws differ from state to state. Different clinics have different policies about confidentiality. Talk to your doctor, call the health department, or call the National AIDS hotline to get your questions answered about testing. If you are 18 or older, your parents will usually not become involved in your decision of whether or not to be tested.

WHAT TO EXPECT WITH HIV TESTING

No matter where you go for an HIV test, you can expect the following: First, the doctor or nurse will probably ask you if you're sure you want to have the test. The results of an STD test have huge physical, social, and emotional implications and can be life-changing. Therefore, you should be prepared to handle the results. Next, the health care professional will either take a blood sample or swab the inside of your cheek. Some offices and clinics can give you your results the same day; others take up to a week or more. While you wait for your results, you should avoid having sexual contact with anyone. If you don't hear from the office or clinic after seven days, give them a call.

WHAT TO DO IF THE RESULTS ARE POSITIVE

If you find out you have a positive HIV test, you will have to talk with a health care professional right away. He or she can advise you on whether or not you need further testing. If a doctor is sure that the positive test means that you are infected with HIV, he or she will give you advice on how to stay healthy and talk to you about medications that can help keep your immune system strong and delay the onset of AIDS. You will need to inform anyone you have had sex with or shared needles with of your diagnosis, so they can decide if they too want to be tested. If you don't feel strong enough to tell people, your doctor or nurse may help you.

IN SUMMARY

Remember that there is no cure for HIV/AIDS, which is why prevention is so important. Antiviral drugs may keep some people healthier longer, but they are unpleasant, and they are not a cure. The best thing you can do to keep yourself healthy and HIV negative is to abstain from sexual intercourse. If you do choose to have sex, be it vaginal, anal, or oral, you should use adequate protection *every time you have sex.*

WHAT YOU NEED TO KNOW

- HIV is the virus that causes AIDS.
- AIDS is a syndrome characterized by a broken immune system, making victims vulnerable to infections and bacteria that healthy people can easily fight off.
- There is no cure for HIV/AIDS.
- The HIV virus can be spread through sexual fluids and blood.
- Many social activities carry no risk of HIV transmission, including cuddling, hugging, closed-mouth or social kissing, and shaking hands.
- Teenagers are just as vulnerable to HIV/AIDS as people of other ages.
- Aside from an HIV test, there is no way to tell if someone is infected with HIV.

➤ Behaviors that put you at an increased risk of HIV include unprotected vaginal, anal, or oral sex; snorting and IV drug use; and getting tattoos or piercings.

➤ Condoms significantly decrease the risk of contracting HIV, but they do not eliminate it; the only way to completely protect yourself is to abstain from sex.

➤ All teenagers who have had sex should be tested at least once for HIV. Some teenagers should have an HIV test once a year. Knowing whether or not you are HIV positive will help you keep yourself and your sexual partners as healthy as possible.

➤ You can go to a family doctor, pediatrician, gynecologist, health department, Planned Parenthood, or an AIDS clinic for an HIV test.

➤ For more information on HIV, call the National AIDS hotlines at (800) 342-AIDS (English) or (800) 344-7432 (Spanish).

9 ▌██ ▐██ ▐██

Human Papillomavirus (HPV)

Human papillomavirus (HPV), a viral infection that can cause warts and cancer, is one of the most common STDs in the United States. It is estimated that approximately 20 million Americans currently have HPV, and about 6.2 million become infected each year. In fact, most sexually active men and women will become infected with HPV at some point in their lives.

If you think you're exempt from HPV in your teenage years, think again. HPV is most common in young men and women; infections usually occur between the ages of 15 and 25, so it is *particularly* important for teenagers to protect themselves against HPV.

Despite being so common, however, HPV is also one of the most poorly understood STDs. The virus is fairly complicated; there are more than 40 types of HPV that can cause a variety of problems—or none at all. When it does cause problems, HPV can lead to genital warts and/or cancer. This chapter will help clear up some of the confusion surrounding HPV and help you prevent HPV infection in yourself and others.

HPV 101

The HPV virus is called the human "papillomavirus" because it tends to cause warts, or papillomas, which are noncancerous tumors. HPV warts usually show up on the genital area.

HPV is usually spread through vaginal, anal, or oral sex, and it can infect the genital areas of both men and women, including the vagina, the vulva (area outside the vagina), the penis, the anus, the cervix (the lower part of the uterus), and the rectum. Most people who become infected with the virus have no symptoms, and therefore, have no idea they have it.

The reason HPV is such a threat is that it has the potential (1) to cause warts on the genitals and (2) to cause cancers of the cervix, vulva, vagina, anus, and penis. HPV is thought to cause 99 percent of genital warts and cervical cancers. The type of HPV that causes warts is different from the type that causes cancer, but both types are currently being passed around the teenage population. The different types of HPV are often split into the categories of "low risk" and "high risk" based on the chance of causing cancer.

There is a new vaccination available that protects against infection with the most common types of wart- and cancer-producing HPV. It is best to get the vaccine before there is any chance of exposure to HPV, which means before you start having sex. The HPV vaccine is now recommended for all girls between 11 and 26 years of age, but it can be given as early as age nine. Researchers are now testing the vaccine in young men, and it may be available for boys in the near future.

HOW HPV SPREADS

HPV infections most often appear in the genital area, anus, and mouth. Although the virus usually spreads through genital contact in the form of vaginal, anal, or oral sex, in rare cases, it can also be passed through hand to genital contact. A British study showed that HPV can be transmitted from one partner's hands to another partner's genitals.

Because HPV often produces no symptoms, infected people can pass the virus onto others without knowing it. HPV can live in the body for years, so a person who contracted the virus a long time ago could still carry it today.

In rare cases, a pregnant woman can pass HPV onto her child during a vaginal delivery. If so, the baby may develop warts in his or her throat, a condition called recurrent respiratory papillomatosis.

SIGNS AND SYMPTOMS OF HPV

About 95 percent of people with HPV do not develop symptoms, but certain types of the virus can cause genital warts in both men and

---

Don't Be Fooled

"HPV? Isn't that something that only girls need to worry about?"
No. The human papillomavirus (HPV) is an STD that affects both men and women. In fact, most sexually active people will have HPV at some point in their lives. About one percent of sexually active men in the United States have genital warts at any given time. High risk forms of HPV, if untreated, can lead to cancers of the penis and anus.

The reason you may think HPV is something that only girls need to worry about is that the virus has made headlines recently with the advent of an HPV vaccine for females ages nine to 26. At this point, there is no approved vaccine for males, but researchers are looking into one. Nor is there a test to look for HPV-related changes in boys and men.

In the meantime, the best way you can protect yourself from HPV is to abstain from having sex. If you do have sex, you can reduce the chance of infection by having sex with only one partner, and by wearing a latex condom correctly every time you have sex. For instructions on how to use a latex condom properly, see Chapter 2, page 27.

---

women, and other forms can cause cancers, including cervical cancer, vulva cancer, and cancers of the vagina, anus, and penis.

Genital warts usually appear as small bumps on the genital area within a few weeks or months of exposure to the virus. Genital warts can be single or multiple, raised or flat, and small or large, and they sometimes appear cauliflower-shaped. Warts usually show up on the vulva, around the vagina or anus, on the thighs, or on the cervix of a female, or on the groin, penis, scrotum, or thigh of a male within a few weeks or months of sexual contact with someone who is infected with HPV.

When left untreated, genital warts may increase in size and number, go away, or stay the same. They will not turn into cancer, and they usually do not cause pain.

Even if you cannot see a wart, HPV can still be there. HPV can cause invisible problems called *squamous intraepithelial lesions* (*SILs*). When a female has a Pap test, the doctor or nurse is testing for SIL on the cervix. SILs can cover the cervix and require a special instrument called a colposcope to be seen. A colposcope is a very specialized microscope that can magnify the cervix so that a doctor can see SILs, even though they may be invisible to the naked eye.

High-risk types of HPV can cause SILs, which can lead to cervical cancer. Symptoms of cervical cancer generally don't show up until the cancer is quite advanced. That's why it's so important for women to get regular Pap tests to screen for cervical cancer.

Other less common cancers that result from high-risk HPV, including cancers of the penis, vulva, vagina, and anus, may also not exhibit signs or symptoms until they are in the later stages. Anal cancer, when it does produce symptoms, causes anal bleeding, pain, itching, or discharge, swollen lymph nodes in the groin or anal area, and a change in bowel habits. Penile cancer may show up as changes in color, skin thickening, or a buildup of tissue on the penis, and later, a growth or sore on the penis.

Luckily, scientists now think that in most cases of both low- and high-risk HPV, the body's immune system clears out the virus on its own within two years, before warts or cancer ever have a chance to develop.

DIAGNOSIS OF HPV

If a teenage girl has ever had sex, even if it was just once, she should talk to her doctor about having regular Pap tests. For females, regular Pap smears can detect changes in the cervix caused by HPV before they turn into cancer. If HPV is detected, there are tests that can determine if the HPV is a low- or high-risk type. If a Pap test reveals cellular changes that signal cervical cancer, your doctor can treat the cancer early, while it is still highly curable.

In addition, whether you are male or female, you should see your health care professional for an examination if you fall into one of the following categories:

> ▸ You have a sexual partner who tells you that he or she has genital warts or genital HPV.
> ▸ You experience itching, bleeding, or pain in your genital area.
> ▸ You notice any unusual bumps or changes on or near your vagina, vulva, anus, or penis.

Your health care professional can diagnose the genital warts caused by HPV through visual inspection. If the warts are flat, some doctors will use a vinegar solution called acetic acid to help identify them. This solution doesn't hurt—it just makes the warts more visible. To find smaller warts, your health care professional may have to use a lighted magnifying lens called a colposcope.

Since syphilis can cause something that looks like warts, you may also need to be tested for syphilis.

HPV Symptoms Chart

Most people with HPV infection do not develop symptoms. But certain types of HPV can cause genital warts, and other forms can cause certain cancers. Here's a quick overview of the symptoms of HPV-related genital warts and cancers.

Genital warts:

▸ Show up within a few weeks or months of sexual contact with an infected person

▸ Usually appear as small bumps or groups of bumps on the vulva, in or around the anus or vagina, on the cervix, on the penis, or on the scrotum, groin, or thigh

▸ Can be raised, flat, small or large, single or multiple, or cauliflower-shaped

▸ May remain unchanged, go away, or increase in size and number if left untreated

▸ Will not turn into cancer

HPV-related cancers, which include cervical cancer, penile cancer, cancer of the vulva, cancer of the vagina, cancer of the anus, and cancer of the penis:

▸ Usually do not show symptoms until they are quite advanced

▸ When symptoms do appear, they sometimes show up as itching, bleeding, swollen lymph nodes, or pain in the affected area

▸ Can be prevented if detected in the precancerous phase and treated

POTENTIAL COMPLICATIONS OF HPV

As mentioned above, HPV comes in two forms—low risk and high risk. The low-risk form may lead to genital warts, and the high-risk form may lead to certain types of cancer.

The high-risk form of HPV may cause normal cells on infected skin to become abnormal. In most cases, the immune system fights off these changes, and the cells go back to normal. If the immune system doesn't clear the high-risk form of HPV, however, it can linger for many years, and the abnormal cells may slowly turn into cancerous ones. Of all the women with high-risk HPV on their cervixes, about 10 percent will develop long-lasting HPV infections that put them at risk for cervical cancer. High-risk HPV can also cause cancer of the penis, anus, vagina, or vulva when it lingers in those areas, but these cancers are much less common than the cervical form.

In terms of statistics, the American Cancer Society (ACS) estimates that in 2008, 11,070 women were diagnosed with cervical cancer. Of the less common types of cancer caused by HPV, the ACS estimated there were 3,460 women diagnosed with cancer of the vulva; 2,210 women diagnosed with vaginal or other female cancers; 1,250 men diagnosed with penile cancer; and 3,050 women and 2,020 men diagnosed with anal cancer. Certain populations of people may be at a greater risk for HPV-related cancers, including individuals with weak immune systems, including those with HIV/AIDS.

TREATMENT

There are no treatments that cure an infection with HPV. Luckily, many people with HPV clear it out of their bodies on their own when they have a strong immune system. To try to boost your immune system—and therefore, help battle an HPV infection if you have one—you can eat a balanced diet, exercise regularly, and avoid cigarettes, alcohol, and drugs.

A small number of not-so-lucky people with HPV, however, will go on to develop warts or cancer.

The goal of treatment for genital warts is to remove visible warts that are annoying and/or embarrassing. To do this, your health care provider may be able to use medication, remove them surgically, use lasers to destroy the warts, or freeze them off. You may also be able to use a patient-applied medication to get rid of the warts.

Keep in mind that treatments for genital warts aren't totally effective; in fact, even with treatment, about 25 percent of people with genital warts have a recurrence within three months. For this reason, some people choose not to have treatment and instead wait to see if the warts clear up on their own.

There are a number of ways to treat precancerous lesions caused by HPV. Treatment will prevent the development of cancer, which is why early detection and treatment is so important.

For cervical cancer and other HPV-related cancers, there are new forms of surgery available, combined with radiation and/or chemotherapy. If a person develops one of these cancers, his or her doctor will discuss their options with them.

HOW TO PROTECT YOURSELF AGAINST HPV

Like other STDs, the only way to completely avoid an HPV infection is to abstain from having sex, be it vaginal, anal, or oral sex. Because HPV often causes no symptoms, it is impossible to tell if a sexual partner has been infected. Therefore, if you do choose to have sex, the safest thing to do is to have sex with only one partner. The more sexual partners you have, the higher your risk for HPV infection.

Beyond abstinence and *monogamy,* here are the best ways to avoid HPV infection:

1. **Get the HPV vaccine.** The first HPV vaccine (Gardasil) was recently approved for young women ages nine to 26. Gardasil helps prevent the four types of HPV that cause most genital warts and 70 percent of cervical cancers. The vaccine is offered to girls at such a young age because ideally, females should be vaccinated before they become sexually active. The vaccine has been tested in more than 11,000 females ages nine to 26 around the world, so experts are confident that it is safe. However, at this time, the vaccine does not protect against all types of HPV that cause cancer and warts (in fact, about 30 percent of cervical cancers and 10 percent of genital warts will not be prevented by the vaccine), and experts don't know how long the vaccine works, so it is important for young females to continue to get regular Pap tests as well. Other HPV vaccines will be available soon, and a vaccine is also being tested in young men, so talk to a health care professional to learn the latest about this new vaccine.
2. **Reduce risk of infection during sex.** Use condoms correctly and consistently. You or your partner should wear

a condom each and every time you have intercourse. For instructions on how to use condoms properly, see Chapter 2, page 27. Keep in mind that condoms are not foolproof, however. Even if you use a condom every time you have sex, you will only cut down your chances of getting HPV by about half. This is because HPV can infect areas not covered by a condom, such as the anus or thighs.

If you're going to have oral sex, do it as safely as possible. Use a condom during oral sex on a male, or a dental dam, a piece of saran wrap, or a split and flattened unlubricated condom during oral sex on a female to provide a barrier between the mouth and the vagina or anus. Also avoid brushing your teeth or flossing immediately after performing oral sex, which may tear your gums and lead to an increased risk of exposure to HPV.

Understand that spermicides in the form of foams, creams, or jellies do not protect against HPV or any other STD. In fact, the FDA has advised against using contraceptives that contain the spermicide nonoxynol-9 because it can increase vaginal irritation, making infection *more* likely.

3. **Females need regular cervical screening for HPV.** If you are female, you should have cervical screening or a Pap test three years after the first time you have sex, and every one to two years after that. If you have been sexually abused as a child or have a weakened immune system, talk to your health care professional; he or she may recommend earlier or more frequent screening. Cervical screening or a Pap test, which can be performed by your gynecologist or regular doctor, will identify unusual or precancerous changes in your cervix. A doctor can remove any abnormal cells before they have a chance to turn into cancer.

During a cervical screening or Pap test, your health care professional will collect cells from your cervix. Although having a pelvic examination and Pap test may be uncomfortable, it should not hurt. The doctor or nurse may then place the cells on a glass slide, which will be sent to a laboratory to be evaluated. There is also a newer Pap test, called the ThinPrep Pap Test, which your doctor may use. During this test, your doctor will place your cervical cells into a fluid-filled vial instead of smearing them onto a slide. If you have a ThinPrep Pap Test, you only have to have it done once every two years (versus once a year if your health care professional uses the conventional glass-slide Pap test).

In certain cases, your doctor may use an HPV DNA test together with a Pap test, which can find high-risk HPV on your cervix. Your doctor should tell you how often you need to be tested after he or she performs this test

No matter which tests he or she uses, if your Pap test results come back as "abnormal," your doctor will recommend some sort of follow-up. He or she may repeat the test after a few months, give you a DNA-based HPV test (if he or she hasn't already), perform a colposcopy, or do a more thorough examination and biopsy of the abnormal area. The most important thing you can do is to follow their recommendations. If you have precancerous lesions, you need treatment so you do not develop cancer.

4. **What about male teenagers?** Unfortunately, there is currently no approved vaccine that helps prevent HPV in males. Studies are underway to find out if a vaccine is safe and effective in men; if it is, the Food and Drug Administration will consider licensing it. There is also no approved routine screening test that looks for HPV-related changes or early signs of penile or anal cancer in males. However, some doctors recommend yearly anal Pap tests for men who have sex with men (MSM), because they are at a higher risk for anal cancer.

WHAT YOU NEED TO KNOW

▶ The human papillomavirus (HPV) is an STD that can lead to genital warts or certain forms of cancer, usually cervical cancer.

▶ HPV infection usually occurs between the ages of 15 and 25, so it is particularly important for teenagers to protect themselves against HPV.

▶ Females between the ages of nine and 26 can have the HPV vaccine to help prevent infection.

▶ There is currently no HPV vaccine approved for males, but researchers are looking into one.

▶ Most people who become infected with HPV have no symptoms, so they have no idea they have it.

▶ The different types of HPV are often split into the categories of "low risk" or "high risk" based on their likelihood of causing cancer.

➤ HPV usually spreads through vaginal, anal, or oral sex, but it can also be passed through hand to genital contact.

➤ Like other STDs, the only way to completely avoid HPV is to abstain from sex.

➤ If you have sex, monogamy (having sex with only one partner) and consistent and correct condom use will lower your chances of HPV infection.

➤ Genital warts usually appear as small bumps on the genital area within a few weeks or months of exposure.

➤ When high-risk HPV leads to cervical cancer, symptoms usually don't show up until the cancer is quite advanced.

➤ Females should talk to a health care professional about Pap tests to screen for HPV-related cervical changes and other STDs when they first become sexually active.

➤ Even with treatment, about 25 percent of people with genital warts will have a recurrence within three months.

➤ Scientists now think that in 90 percent of HPV cases, the body's immune system eliminates the virus within two years.

10

Syphilis

Syphilis is an infection that has plagued people through out history. In the 16th through 19th centuries, syphilis ran wild. And without an effective treatment, many cases of syphilis entered the later stages, causing damage to major organ systems, insanity, blindness, and in some cases, death. In the past, the late stage of syphilis was one of the most common causes of dementia—which means people become (and stay) confused and disoriented. It affected numerous famous people, including Al Capone, King Edward VI of England, the painter Edouard Manet, and the composer Ludwig van Beethoven.

Luckily, thanks to modern medicine, scientists have discovered a cure for syphilis that works quite well if the infection is caught in the earlier stages. Today, instead of facing blindness or insanity, you can get tested for syphilis with a simple blood test, and if you are infected, you can get treated with antibiotics and become completely cured. In fact, penicillin has been effectively used in the treatment of syphilis for more than 50 years.

A few decades ago, syphilis was thought to be an STD of the past. In 2000 syphilis rates reached the lowest point since reporting began in 1941. But unfortunately, this STD seems to be making a comeback. Between 2001 and 2007, the rate of syphilis began to rise again. The fastest rise seems to be taking place in men (the number of cases rose from 3.0 cases per 100,000 in 2001 to 6.6 cases per 100,000 in 2007). And after a decline since 1990, rates of syphilis in women rose from 0.8 cases per 100,000 in 2004 to 1.1 case per 100,000 in 2007. Between the years 2006 and 2007, the total number of cases of syphilis (all primary and secondary stages of the disease, and in both men and women) increased more than 15 percent.

The recent rise in syphilis isn't limited to the United States. The World Health Organization estimated that there were 100,000 new cases of syphilis in North America in 1999, 140,000 new cases in Western Europe, 100,000 in Eastern Europe and Central Asia, 370,000 in North Africa and the Middle East, and three to four million each in Latin America, the Caribbean, sub-Saharan Africa, and south and southeast Asia.

The point is that while syphilis may have faded as a threat a few decades ago, it's now one of the STDs that adults and teenagers face.

SYPHILIS 101

Syphilis is a sexually transmitted disease (STD) caused by the *Treponema pallidum* bacterium, a type of very small bacteria called a spirochete, which is shaped like a corkscrew or spiral. Syphilis is often called "The Great Imitator," because its symptoms mimic those caused by numerous other diseases and conditions.

There are a few different stages of syphilis—primary, secondary, latent, and late (tertiary). If any one stage of syphilis goes untreated, it may move to the next subsequent stage.

The primary stage of syphilis usually sets in between 10 and 90 days (21 days, on average) from the initial infection, and it typically shows up as a single or multiple sores at the site of infection. The sores then ulcerate to produce *chancres*, small ulcers one to two centimeters in size. These chancres usually heal within three to six weeks.

A skin rash and/or areas of abnormal tissue on the skin or mucous membranes usually signal the secondary stage of syphilis, which generally sets in within a few weeks of the primary stage. Other symptoms of the secondary stage may include fever, swollen lymph glands, sore throat, headaches, and weight loss, among others.

During the next stage of syphilis, the latent (hidden) stage, all symptoms disappear. The syphilis infection remains in the body, however, and without treatment, this quiet stage will move into the later, more serious stage. In the late stage of syphilis, the infection may damage internal organs, including the brain, nerves, heart, blood vessels, and eyes. In some cases, it may eventually lead to death.

As an important side note, syphilis makes HIV infection more likely, because the chancres associated with syphilis can give the HIV virus a quick route of transmission into the body. In the 6,862 syphilis infections that occurred in 2002, according to the Centers for Disease Control and Prevention (CDC), 25 percent of them took place in people who also had HIV. If you have been exposed to syphilis, your chances of HIV infection are two to five times higher than a person who is syphilis-free.

HOW SYPHILIS SPREADS

Syphilis spreads from person to person by way of direct contact with a syphilis sore. Sores occur mainly on the vagina, anus, rectum, or penis, but they can also appear on the mouth or lips. These sores, as well as the mucous lesions that can occur as a result of secondary syphilis infection, are highly contagious. If you come in contact with a syphilis sore or lesion through direct exposure from an infected person, chances are one in three that you too will become infected.

Exposure to syphilis sores or lesions usually occurs as a result of vaginal, anal, or oral sex with someone who is infected. You can also contract syphilis through kissing or touching a person if he or she has active chancres or lesions on the mouth, lips, breasts, or genitals.

Unfortunately, syphilis chancres are not always obvious; therefore, a person may have syphilis sores hidden in his or her vagina, rectum, or mouth and pass the infection onto you without even knowing they have it.

Pregnant women with syphilis can also pass it onto their babies, where the infection can cause serious birth defects. You cannot get syphilis via toilet seats, swimming pools, hot tubs, doorknobs, bathtubs, or utensils.

SIGNS AND SYMPTOMS OF SYPHILIS

As mentioned, syphilis has often been referred to as "the great imitator," because its symptoms mimic those of so many other diseases. And like other STDs, syphilis sometimes produces no symptoms at all.

Primary syphilis. The first symptom of the primary stage of syphilis is usually the appearance of a sore or sores at the initial site of infection, be it the genitals, anus, or mouth. These sores usually show up within a few weeks of infection, and they are generally small, firm, round, and painless. In some cases, they are wet. After the sores appear, they soon ulcerate to form chancres.

Syphilis is highly contagious at this primary stage. The chancres last for about three to six weeks, and they will heal without treatment. However, if the proper treatment isn't administered in the primary stage, the infection will progress to the secondary stage in about 25 percent of untreated people.

Secondary syphilis. Symptoms of the secondary stage of syphilis may include a skin rash and lesions on the mucous membranes, such as the vagina, perineum (area between the genitals and the anus), or mouth. The secondary stage usually starts with the rash, which can show up on the body, arms, or legs (usually the palms of the hands and the soles of the feet) while chancres are healing or several weeks after they have healed. The rash may appear rough, red, or reddish with brown spots, and it will usually be painless. Sometimes these rashes are so faint that those suffering from the secondary stage of syphilis don't even notice them.

In addition to skin rashes and lesions, people in the secondary stage of syphilis may have a fever, swollen lymph glands, patchy hair loss, a sore throat, weight loss, headaches, muscle aches, and tiredness. Syphilis is still very contagious during the secondary stage. Similarly to the primary stage, the signs and symptoms of secondary syphilis will usually resolve themselves within a few weeks without treatment, but this lack of treatment may cause the infection to progress to the latent or late stage.

Latent syphilis. During the latent (or "hidden") stage of syphilis, which can last for years, all signs and symptoms cease, but the infection still lives in the body. Many people with syphilis never progress beyond this stage, but about 15 percent will move onto the dangerous late stage of syphilis, which may not show up until 10 to 20 years after the initial infection.

Late syphilis. In the late stage of syphilis (also known as the tertiary stage), the spirochete bacteria spread all over the body, affecting multiple organs and systems. Signs and symptoms of the late stage include paralysis, coordination problems (difficulty moving), numbness, blindness, and dementia (loss of mental capacity that may affect memory, language, attention, and personality) as the infection damages the internal organs. Specifically, syphilis attacks the brain, nerves, eyes, liver, bones, joints, heart, and blood vessels. The damage caused by the infection can be severe enough to lead to death.

SYPHILIS DIAGNOSIS

Because syphilis produces signs and symptoms that so closely resemble those of other diseases and conditions, it is a hard STD for doctors to recognize. If syphilis is in the primary or secondary stage and is producing sores, a health care professional may be able to diagnose the infection by examining secretions from one of the chancres under a special microscope called a dark-field microscope.

Syphilis can also be diagnosed through a blood test. Soon after infection with syphilis bacteria, the body starts to produce syphilis antibodies; a blood test can detect these antibodies and therefore determine whether or not a person has indeed been infected. Because the infection can be so serious for a developing baby, all pregnant women are advised to take a syphilis blood test early in their pregnancies.

In cases where syphilis has progressed to the latent stage, health care professionals will look for signs of late or tertiary syphilis. Specifically, they may look at the heart for evidence of murmurs, or examine the eyes for any signs of syphilis-related eye disease. If a health care professional indeed suspects tertiary syphilis, he or she may order further tests on the heart, eyes, and other areas of the body.

TREATMENT OF SYPHILIS

When it is caught in the early stages—the primary or secondary stage—syphilis is relatively easy to treat. If you have had syphilis for less than a year, a single injection of the antibiotic penicillin will take care of the infection.

If you are allergic to penicillin, you may be able to take other antibiotics in its place. Health care professionals occasionally use the antibiotics doxycycline and azithromycin to treat syphilis, which are safe in most people allergic to penicillin.

If you have had syphilis for longer than a year, you may need additional injections of antibiotics. The spirochete bacteria involved in syphilis infection evolve and grow stronger over time, so the longer they live, the higher the doses of antibiotics required to kill them. And although antibiotics can stop the infection from getting worse, they cannot undo any damage that syphilis has already done to the body.

Even if you don't discover or address a syphilis infection until it reaches the later stages, you will be treated with antibiotics. Treatment at the later stage will prevent the infection from doing further damage to your body and could save your life.

During treatment for a syphilis infection, you will have to abstain from sexual contact until a doctor or nurse tells you it is safe to have sex again. In the meantime, you should notify all former sexual partners of your infection, so they too can get tested.

After you have been treated for a syphilis infection, your health care professional will want to see you again for follow-up visits for at least 12 months after your initial treatment. During these visits, he or

Symptom Chart

Primary syphilis: A single sore or chancre appears within 10 to 90 days of the initial infection; the chancre may be single or multiple. Chancres usually appear firm, round, sometimes wet, and small, and they are painless. Chancres generally last three to six weeks and heal without treatment—even though you are still infected. If the infection isn't treated, it may progress to the secondary stage

Secondary syphilis: Symptoms of secondary syphilis are sometimes so faint that they aren't noticed. A skin rash shows up on the body, arms, or legs, usually on the palms of the hands and soles of the feet. The rash may look rough, red, or appear as reddish brown spots; it doesn't itch. These rashes may closely resemble those caused by other conditions and diseases that can fool doctors and nurses, so tell them you need to be tested for syphilis if you may be infected. Lesions may appear on mucous membranes, including the mouth, vagina, and perineum (area between the genitals and anus). Flu-like symptoms may set in, including fever, swollen lymph glands, sore throat, hair loss, headaches, muscle aches, tiredness, and weight loss. Symptoms usually resolve on their own; but without treatment, you are still infected and syphilis is likely to progress to the latent and then possibly the later stages.

Latent (hidden) stage: Begins when symptoms of primary and secondary syphilis disappear. No signs or symptoms are present, but the infection stays active in the body. Latent stage can last for years.

Late (tertiary) stage: About 15 percent of people who have not been treated move to the late stage. Late stage syphilis may damage internal organs, including the brain, nerves, eyes, heart, blood vessels, bones, liver, and joints. Damage leads to paralysis, numbness, difficulty coordinating muscles, blindness, dementia, and possibly death.

she will probably perform a visual inspection to make sure all sores and signs of syphilis are gone, as well as repeat any blood work to make sure the bacteria is completely out of your system. About 15 percent of people are not syphilis-free a year after treatment and have to be retreated. If you think you may need to be retreated for syphilis at any point, talk to your health care professional.

Unfortunately, having syphilis once will not protect you from another infection down the line. Once you've had a syphilis infection and received treatment, you are just as vulnerable to infection as someone who has never had it.

HOW TO PROTECT YOURSELF FROM SYPHILIS

Like other STDs, the surest way to avoid syphilis is to abstain from having sex, be it vaginal, anal, or oral sex. The second best way to avoid infection is to stay in a monogamous relationship with a person you are certain does not have syphilis. Beyond that, here are some things you can do to protect yourself:

Limit your number of sexual partners. If you are not in a monogamous relationship, the fewer your sexual partners, the lower your chances of contracting syphilis.

Steer clear of drugs and alcohol. Alcohol and drugs lower your inhibitions, making you more likely to engage in risky sexual behaviors that may put you at risk for syphilis.

Use condoms consistently and correctly. When used properly every time you engage in vaginal sexual intercourse, latex condoms can lower your chances of a syphilis infection by about half. For information on how to use condoms properly, see Chapter 2, page 27. Syphilis chancres can show up on areas of both the male and female body that are not protected or covered by a condom. Therefore, you can use a condom and still pass on or contract syphilis.

Address symptoms or concerns immediately. The sooner you catch a syphilis infection, the faster and more effectively you can be treated, so you should see your health care professional right away if you think you might have been exposed to syphilis or if you experience any symptoms of the infection, including an unusual sore, discharge, or rash. In the meantime, you should refrain from any sexual activities.

Don't Be Fooled

"I thought I may have had an STD, but the symptoms went away, so I must be OK."

Wrong. Many STDs don't exhibit any symptoms at all, so you could easily be infected and not know it. And in the case of syphilis, the infection usually produces symptoms in the early stages, and they then disappear for a while in the latent stage, which can last for years.

More specifically, in the primary stage of syphilis, sores may show up at the site of infection. A few weeks later, you may develop a rash, lesions on mucous membranes such as the mouth and vagina, and flu-like symptoms such as a fever, swollen glands, headaches, sore throat, and weight loss. After these symptoms of initial infection disappear, which they often do on their own without treatment, the infection goes into a latent stage, where it produces no symptoms but still remains very much alive in the body.

Moreover, you should never assume that an STD has gone away simply because your symptoms have disappeared. If you suspect you may have an STD—either because of symptoms or because you fear you may have had sex with someone who is infected—go see your health care professional right away. Getting tested and treated is easy, and you can be cured with antibiotics. The sooner you receive treatment for an STD like syphilis, the better your chances will be for a full recovery.

Get tested regularly. Because it is sometimes very difficult to spot syphilis chancres, if you are having sex, you should get tested for syphilis on a regular basis, especially if you have had unprotected sex or sex with more than one partner.

If you are a man having sex with men (MSM), be aware of your increased risk for syphilis. Syphilis rates have increased in all demographic groups over the past few years, but the spike has been particularly pronounced in MSM, especially in the areas of Chicago, Seattle, San Francisco, Miami, New York City, and Southern California. And high rates of HIV infection have been reported in 20 to 70 percent of these syphilis cases; therefore, MSM should be aware of their increased risk of both infections and be extremely careful about protecting themselves and their partners. Get tested at least once a year.

WHAT YOU NEED TO KNOW

▶ A few decades ago, syphilis was thought to be an STD of the past. But starting in 2001, rates of the bacterial infection began to rise again.

▶ There are a few different stages of syphilis—primary, secondary, latent, and late (tertiary).

▶ The primary stage of syphilis typically sets in between 10 and 90 days from the initial infection and manifests as a single or multiple sores (or chancres) at the site of infection.

▶ The secondary stage of syphilis usually shows up as a skin rash and/or lesions on mucous membranes.

▶ A fever, swollen lymph nodes, a sore throat, headaches, and weight loss may also accompany the secondary stage.

▶ During the latent stage, all symptoms disappear, but the infection remains in the body.

▶ In the late stage of syphilis, the infection may damage internal organs and eventually lead to death.

▶ Syphilis makes HIV infection more likely.

▶ Syphilis spreads from person to person by way of direct contact, usually through vaginal, anal, or oral sex.

▶ The best way to prevent syphilis is to abstain from sex.

▶ Following abstinence, the best things you can do are stay in a monogamous relationship with someone you know is syphilis-free and use condoms consistently and correctly.

▶ Condoms are not totally effective in preventing syphilis; even when used properly, they only cut down the risk of infection by half.

▶ If you come into direct contact with a syphilis sore or lesion, chances are one in three that you will become infected.

▶ Syphilis sores aren't always obvious; therefore, you or someone else can be infected without realizing it.

▶ When caught in the primary or secondary stages, syphilis is easy to treat with antibiotics, usually penicillin.

▶ Having syphilis once will not protect you from infection down the line.

▶ The sooner syphilis is caught, the more effectively it can be treated, so you should see your health care professional right away if you experience any symptoms or suspect you may have been infected.

➤ Getting tested for syphilis is easy. You can usually get tested with a simple blood test.

➤ Syphilis can be cured with the right antibiotics.

Vaginitis

From a longer life expectancy to the joys of carrying a child, there are many benefits to being female. Unfortunately, when it comes to STDs, there are also some downsides. One downside is having a particular propensity to developing vaginal infections, or vaginitis. It's normal to have some vaginal discharge. In fact, vaginal discharge is necessary to clean and moisten the vagina, as well as to help prevent and fight infection. Although your discharge may change slightly throughout your menstrual cycle, from thin to sticky to elastic, normally it should appear clear or whitish with little odor, and it should not cause irritation.

Abnormal vaginal discharge, on the other hand, is discharge that causes irritation or itching, has a strong odor, or contains some blood or appears to be frothy, gray and milky, or yellow-green. This is a common symptom of vaginitis.

THE "BIG THREE" TYPES OF VAGINITIS

The three most common forms of vaginitis are yeast infections, trichomoniasis, and bacterial vaginosis. Although their symptoms are similar, each type of vaginitis is caused by its own set of pathogens, and therefore must be treated differently. It is also possible to have more than one of these three types of vaginitis at one time, which is sometimes classified as a "mixed type infection."

1. *Yeast infections:* Yeast infections can cause a vaginal discharge that is very thick and white, like cottage cheese. A yeast infection will usually not cause a strong odor, but it may cause intense itching and burning.
2. *Trichomoniasis:* Trichomoniasis causes discharge that has a musty, stale odor and is grayish or yellow-green in color. Trichomoniasis also frequently causes vaginal itching and burning during urination.
3. *Bacterial vaginosis (BV):* BV causes a discharge that is heavier than usual. The discharge often has an unpleasant fishy odor and is foamy or frothy and grayish in color.

These are the "classic" symptoms, but if a young woman is having symptoms of vaginitis, it is impossible for her to know which infection(s) she has unless she is tested by a doctor or nurse. If you suspect you may have any of the above infections because you are having symptoms, or because you know or suspect that a partner is infected, see your doctor—either your pediatrician or family doctor or gynecologist—as soon as possible. If you'd rather not make an appointment with your doctor, you can also go to a local reproductive health clinic, such as Planned Parenthood.

Here are some more details about each infection.

YEAST VAGINITIS

Yeast infections are not related to sex, and they are not considered STDs, so we will not go into detail about yeast infections in this book. But it is important to mention yeast infections, because they are a common cause of vaginal discharge, itching, and burning. It is impossible for a young woman with an unusual vaginal discharge to know if the discharge is being caused by yeast, trichomoniasis, or BV. Only a health care professional can make the diagnosis after an examination. If your exam reveals that you have a yeast infection, it can be treated and cured. Because it is not an STD, your partner will not need to be treated for a yeast infection. Your doctor or nurse will tell you more.

TRICHOMONIASIS

Trichomoniasis or trich (pronounced "trik") is a common curable sexually transmitted disease (STD) that may cause unpleasant vaginal discharge, itching, and odor in girls. Although males can carry it too, it seldom causes symptoms in them.

Trichomoniasis is caused by a protozoan called *Trichomonas vaginalis* that can live in the urogenital tract of both males and females. In females, the infection usually shows up in the vagina; in males, it usually infects the urethra (urine canal). Trich can infect any person who is sexually active, but it shows up more frequently in people who have more than one sexual partner or who do not use protection during sex.

Despite how common it is, trichomoniasis doesn't get the same attention as other STDs that occur in teenagers, such as chlamydia, HPV, and gonorrhea.

How trichonomiasis spreads. Trichomoniasis most commonly spreads through sexual contact, particularly if that sex is unprotected. Females can catch the infection from infected males or females, but males usually contract it from females only.

Because trichomoniasis can survive for short periods of time in moist environments, in theory you could get the protozoan from contaminated items or surfaces, such as wet towels or bathing suits. These methods of transmission are rare, however.

Symptoms of trichomoniasis. Once you have been infected, symptoms of trichomoniasis can show up as early as four days later, or as late as 28 days or more after exposure. However, some people experience no symptoms at all (about one-third of women and about 90 percent of men have no symptoms), so the infection often goes undiagnosed and untreated.

In females, symptoms may include:

> ➤ An unusual frothy, watery, or milky discharge ranging in color from green to gray to yellow
> ➤ Foul odor
> ➤ Soreness and/or itching in or around the vagina
> ➤ Pain during urination
> ➤ Pain during sex
> ➤ Bleeding after sex
> ➤ Itching or soreness of the labia and/or inner thighs
> ➤ Swollen labia
> ➤ Abdominal pain

Males with trichomoniasis usually don't have symptoms, but when they do, symptoms may include:

> Painful or difficult urination
> Itching of the urethra (the tube through which urine and semen are discharged)
> Burning after urination or ejaculation
> Painful and inflamed scrotum
> Inflammation of the prostate gland
> Frothy or pus-like discharge from the urethra

Diagnosis of trichomoniasis. Because its symptoms mimic those of so many other conditions, especially yeast infections and bacterial vaginosis (BV), you should not try to self-diagnose trichomoniasis.

If you think you may have trichomoniasis because you are having symptoms or because you know or suspect that a partner is infected, see your doctor—your pediatrician, family doctor, or gynecologist—as soon as possible. If you'd rather not make an appointment with your doctor, you can also go to a local heath department or a reproductive health clinic, such as Planned Parenthood.

If you are a female, the doctor will determine whether or not you have a trichomoniasis infection by taking a sample of your vaginal discharge. During the exam, the doctor may also notice small red sores on the cervix or walls of the vagina.

In general, trich is easier to diagnose in females than in males. Some doctors will test males by swabbing the inside of the urethra. But because such a high percentage of male partners of females with trichomoniasis have the infection themselves—up to 70 percent—doctors should give male partners medication to treat the infection without confirming that they actually have it.

If you want your health care professional to test you for trichomoniasis, you will have to ask for the test specifically. Do not assume that your doctor will automatically test you for trichomoniasis and other STDs at your annual screening exam.

You may get a diagnosis immediately if the doctor or nurse can identify trichomoniasis under the microscope in the clinic. In some cases, it will take a few days for your test results to come back. Some doctors' offices and clinics are now offering a rapid results test called the OSOM Trichomonas Rapid Test that they can read in as little as 10 minutes. If you are in a hurry for your results, ask your doctor if this test is a possibility for you.

At your doctor's appointment, you will want to gather as much information about trichomoniasis—and protecting your sexual health in general—as you can. To make the most of your appointment, prepare a list of questions to ask ahead of time. Here are some specific questions you may want to consider:

> Can I treat trichomoniasis with yeast infection medication?
> What are the telltale symptoms of trichomoniasis?
> Can I get this infection again?
> What can I do to prevent trichomoniasis in the future?
> Are there any dangerous side effects of the medications used to treat trichomoniasis?
> Does my partner need to be treated?
> Do I need to be tested for other STDs and HIV?

Treatment of trichomoniasis. If you and your doctor discover that you indeed have a trichomoniasis infection, you will be treated with specific prescription antibiotic medications, either metronidazole (Flagyl or generic) or tinidazole (Tindamax), which you will probably take in a single oral dose. If you are pregnant, the doctor will decide which is safest for you.

If you have trich, you should notify anyone with whom you had sex in the past 60 days of your infection, so he or she can seek treatment. Keep in mind that symptoms of trichomoniasis may disappear completely after about 10 days in a male, even though he still has the infection and can pass it back to a previous partner or on to a new partner. Therefore, all male partners of infected females should get treatment for the infection, both for their own protection and the protection of their sexual partners.

While you are being treated for trichomoniasis, both you and your partner(s) should avoid all sexual activity. And keep in mind that, unfortunately, having trichomoniasis once will not protect you from getting it again; in fact, reinfection is quite common in teenagers.

In most cases—about 90 to 95 percent—metronidazole or tinidazole antibiotics work to completely cure a trichomoniasis infection. If your symptoms clear up, you do not have to see your doctor again for a follow-up visit. If you still experience symptoms, however, and five to 10 percent of women do, you may need a longer course of the medication. Keep in mind that both drugs used to treat trichomoniasis can cause a nasty reaction of nausea and vomiting when mixed with alcohol, so avoid drinking alcohol while taking these medications and for three days afterward.

While you are being treated for trichomoniasis, ask your doctor to test you for other STDs and HIV. If you have been diagnosed with trichomoniasis, you are automatically at a higher risk for other STDs. And because these STDs often have no symptoms, the only way to know for sure whether or not you have them is to be tested.

Potential complications of trichomoniasis. Overall, trichomoniasis is a highly treatable STD. If it goes untreated, however, trich can increase a female's risk of HIV should she be exposed to the virus. A trich infection will also make it more likely that a female will pass HIV onto a sexual partner.

In addition, trichomoniasis can cause complications in pregnancy. A pregnant female with the infection may have a baby who is born too early (before 37 weeks) or at a low birth weight (less than 5.5 pounds). In fact, research has shown that women with trichomoniasis are 40 percent more likely to have a low birth weight baby than those without the infection.

If trichomoniasis goes untreated in males, it can lead to an infection of the urethra. Plus, an untreated male is always at risk of infecting his female partners.

Prevention. As with most STDs, the only way to completely prevent trichomoniasis is to abstain from having sex. If you do have sex, you should do so in a mutually monogamous relationship, meaning that both you and your partner have sex only with each other and no one else. Beyond that, here are some other actions you can take to help prevent trichomoniasis: Use a latex condom consistently and correctly every time you have sex. Natural membrane condoms don't provide as much protection as latex condoms. And keep in mind that even latex condoms do not provide 100 percent protection. For instructions on how to properly use condoms, see Chapter 2, page 27.

Do not douche. Although some teenage girls douche because they think it improves their genital hygiene, actually, the opposite is true. The vagina has been called "self-cleaning," and this metaphor is accurate. The vagina naturally makes acids that help keep unhealthy bacteria in check. Douching can actually disrupt these acids, therefore changing the natural flora of the vagina. And physically, douching can flush bacteria higher into your genital tract. Both effects actually increase your risk of contracting an STD like trichomoniasis.

Don't share towels or swimsuits. Although the chances of getting trichomoniasis any way other than having unprotected sex are rare, because the parasite can live outside the body, it is possible to contract it after contact with an infected damp or moist object. To be on the safe side, avoid sharing towels, bathing suits, or other damp items (moisture helps keep the parasite alive) with anyone.

Do not rely on *hormonal birth control* methods to protect you. Latex condoms are the only birth control methods that help protect against trichomoniasis and other STDs. Other forms of birth control, such as birth control pills, diaphragms, implants, or shots, will help prevent pregnancy, but they are powerless against STDs.

Pay attention to your body. As soon as you experience any unusual genital symptoms, such as an abnormal discharge, a rash, or burning during urination, stop having sex and see a health care professional right away.

Get regular physical exams. These exams should include STD screening. As mentioned, because many STDs common in teens produce no symptoms, the only way of knowing for sure whether or not you have one is to be tested. In addition, you may want to talk with your health care professional about sexual health issues in general. These professionals can answer any questions you have about STDs and what puts you at risk.

BACTERIAL VAGINOSIS

Bacterial vaginosis, or BV, is a very common vaginal infection in women of childbearing age but the most poorly understood. Of the three types of vaginitis—yeast infections, trichomoniasis, and bacterial vaginosis—BV is the most common, and it is a unique threat to females. The organisms that cause BV cannot survive in the male urethra.

Sexually active females are much more likely to get bacterial vaginosis (BV), but it is possible to contract the infection if you have never have sex, so BV is not an STD in the true sense of the word.

Although the exact cause of BV is unknown, it seems to result from an overgrowth of certain bacteria in the vagina. This overgrowth usually results from a disruption in the normal vaginal bacterial balance between "good" and "bad" bacteria; the bad bacteria take over, causing abnormal discharge, pain, itching, burning, and unpleasant odor.

More specifically, in a healthy vagina, about 95 percent of the bacteria belong to a class called *lactobacillus.* There are several different types of lactobacillus, at least one of which keeps the vagina's pH at a normal level. When this normal level becomes unbalanced, the bad microorganisms can take over, leading to an infection and abnormal discharge—BV. Unfortunately, once this imbalance occurs, it's difficult for a woman's body to get it back to normal.

Exactly how women get BV is a bit of a mystery. But because BV may lead to significant health complications, it is starting to get more attention. BV has been linked to all of the following: pelvic inflammatory disease (PID); complications after reproductive surgeries like abortion and cesarean section; increased risk of HIV; and potentially, infertility.

Despite the mystery surrounding BV, it is common in the United States, accounting for about 17–19 percent of family planning or student health clinic visits and 24–37 percent of STD clinic visits. BV is particularly prevalent in pregnant women; as many as one-third of pregnant women in the United States have the infection.

How BV spreads. Experts aren't sure exactly how women get bacterial vaginosis, since it occurs both in females who are sexually active and those who are not. There are some behaviors, however, that upset the normal balance of bacteria in the vagina and, therefore, seem to make BV more likely. These activities include having a new sex partner, having multiple sexual partners, and douching. Despite what some people think, you *cannot* get bacterial vaginosis from toilet seats, swimming pools, bed linens, or by touching objects around you.

Symptoms of BV. Many females with bacterial vaginosis—about 50–75 percent—experience no symptoms at all, so it is quite possible that you could have the infection and not know it. When symptoms do occur, they usually include one or more of the following:

▸ A strong fish-like odor. This odor may become particularly strong after sexual intercourse because semen changes the acidic level of the vaginal fluids.
▸ Unusual gray or white vaginal discharge; it may be thin and resemble skim milk
▸ Burning during urination
▸ Itching around the outside of the vagina

Diagnosis of BV. If you suspect you may have bacterial vaginosis, see your doctor. He or she will look at your vagina for signs of BV and take a sample of fluid to look for any bacteria associated with the condition. Specifically, your health care professional will take your discharge specimen and examine it under a microscope for "clue cells"—cells from the vagina that are covered with bacteria.

Keep in mind that the Papanicolaou smear (Pap smear) that you get at your annual gynecological exam is not a reliable test for BV, and your health care professional will not test you automatically. If you suspect you may have BV, you should clearly ask for a test for the condition.

Treatment of BV. Although bacterial vaginosis sometimes clears up on its own without treatment, if you have symptoms, you should seek treatment; untreated BV can lead to complications. Luckily, in most cases, treatment works to restore the correct balance of good to bad bacteria in the vagina and, therefore, to cure BV.

If your doctor finds that you indeed have BV, he or she will likely prescribe metronidazole (Flagyl or generic) or clindamycin (Clindamycin). Both metronidazole and clindamycin are available in a gel that you insert into your vagina or a pill. Clindamycin is usually reserved for cases of BV that don't respond to metronidazole.

If you are taking metronidazole (either the oral or vaginal form), avoid drinking any alcohol while you are taking the medication and for three days after because it may cause severe nausea and vomiting. Also keep in mind that the gel form of clindamycin may weaken condoms and make them ineffective.

Because it is specifically a female condition, your male sexual partner(s) will not need to be treated for BV. If you have a female partner, however, she will need treatment.

Treatment for BV is particularly important for pregnant women because BV has been linked to pregnancy complications, such as low birth weight (less than 5.5 pounds) and premature delivery (before 37 weeks). All pregnant women who have ever had a premature delivery or a baby with a low birth weight should talk to their doctor about testing for BV, whether they have symptoms or not. If BV is found, they should be treated. Pregnant women can take either metronidazole or clindamycin, but the dosages will be different than those for nonpregnant females.

In addition to prescription medications, researchers are looking into ways women can prevent BV by keeping the levels of their healthy vaginal bacteria in check, such as eating more yogurt, which contains the healthy bacteria, or taking the bacteria in a capsule form.

While you are being treated for BV, avoid any kind of sexual contact. And if you develop BV three or more times in one year, talk to your health care professional about using prophylactic medication (medication that you use on a regular basis to prevent BV).

Unfortunately, BV recurs after treatment in about 25 percent of women. If your symptoms continue after you have finished your medication, or if they show up again a few weeks or months later, call your doctor.

At your doctor's appointment, you will want to gather as much information about bacterial vaginosis as you can. To make the most of your appointment, prepare a list of questions to ask ahead of time. Here are some specific questions you may want to consider:

▸ Are there any over-the-counter products that work to prevent BV?
▸ Does my partner need to be treated (male or female)?

➤ What is the difference between BV and a yeast infection?
➤ How can I avoid BV in the future?
➤ What are the signs and symptoms of BV so I can recognize it if it occurs again?
➤ Should I refrain from all sexual contact while I am being treated?
➤ Can I douche if I only do it now and then?
➤ Is BV considered a sexually transmitted disease?

Potential complications of BV. In most cases, BV causes no complications. It can cause problems in some females, however, including an increased risk of contracting HIV if one is exposed, and an increased risk of passing HIV onto a partner; a higher risk of infection following genital surgical procedures, such as abortion; a higher chance of contracting other STDs, such as herpes simplex virus, gonorrhea, or chlamydia; an increased risk of complications in pregnancy, including low birth weight (less than 5.5 pounds) or premature birth (before 37 weeks); and a higher risk of pelvic inflammatory disease (PID), an infection that can cause damage of the fallopian tubes that increases a woman's risk for *ectopic pregnancy* and/or infertility.

Preventing BV. Because experts aren't exactly sure how bacterial vaginosis spreads, the best ways to prevent it remain a mystery. However, the following actions may reduce your chances of getting the infection: **Abstain from having sex.** Although it is possible to get BV without being sexually active, having sex increases your chances significantly.

Limit your number of sexual partners. For reasons that aren't exactly clear, the more sexual partners you have, the higher your chances for getting BV.

If you are sexually active, use condoms. You should use condoms correctly any time you engage in sexual activity to prevent all STDs, including BV. Condoms are effective against BV because they protect the inside of the vagina from semen, which can affect the vaginal bacteria balance. For instructions on how to properly use condoms, see Chapter 2, page 27.

Don't douche. The vagina naturally makes acids that help keep unhealthy bacteria in check, and douching can actually disrupt these acids, thereby changing the natural flora of the vagina. And physically, douching can flush bacteria higher into your genital tract. Both effects actually increase your risk for BV. In fact, researchers at Michigan State University found that douching may as much as triple a woman's risk of BV.

Symptom Chart

The following symptoms may indicate that you have trichomoniasis or bacterial vaginosis (BV):

Trichomoniasis

Females

> ▸ An unusual frothy, watery, or milky discharge ranging in color from green to gray to yellow

> ▸ Unpleasant odor

> ▸ Soreness and/or itching in or around the vagina

> ▸ Pain during urination

> ▸ Pain during sex

> ▸ Bleeding after sex

> ▸ Itching or soreness of the labia and/or inner thighs

> ▸ Swollen labia

> ▸ Abdominal pain

Keep your vagina natural. In addition to douching, other products that claim to keep you "fresh" may actually do the opposite by disrupting the healthy pH in your vagina, thus making BV more likely. These products include deodorant tampons and feminine hygiene sprays.

If you have BV, finish all the medication your doctor prescribes for you. If your symptoms go away early, you may be tempted to stop taking your medication, but you should finish all of the antibiotics prescribed by your doctor, no matter if your symptoms subside or not.

Have regular check-ups. Yearly checkups provide you the opportunity to be tested for STDs and ask your health care professional about conditions like BV. Talk to your doctor about how often you should have a pelvic exam and which additional tests you should have.

Males
- Painful or difficult urination
- Itching of the urethra (the tube through which urine and semen are discharged)
- Burning after urination or ejaculation
- Painful and inflamed scrotum
- Inflammation of the prostate gland
- Frothy or pus-like discharge from the urethra

Bacterial vaginosis
- Abnormal vaginal discharge with an unpleasant "fishy" odor
- Odor that worsens after sexual intercourse
- Discharge that is milky, white, or gray and thin
- Burning during urination
- Itching around the outside of the vagina
- Vaginal irritation

WHAT YOU NEED TO KNOW
- All females have some vaginal discharge, but when discharge causes irritation or itching, has a strong odor, contains some blood, or appears frothy, gray and milky, or yellow-green, a diagnosis is in order.
- Both trichomoniasis and bacterial vaginosis are particularly troublesome vaginal infections for females.
- Trichomoniasis is a STD caused by a parasite; although it can occur in males, it is more common in females.
- Bacterial vaginosis (BV) is a disruption in the bacteria naturally found in the vagina that is totally unique to females.

- BV can spread through sexual contact, but it also sometimes occurs in females who have never had sex. So it is not a true STD.
- About one-third of women and 90 percent of men have no symptoms with trichomoniasis.
- About 50 to 75 percent of females with BV experience no symptoms.
- Do not try to self-diagnose trichomoniasis or BV. If you suspect you may have one of these infections, see your doctor.
- Do not assume that your doctor will test you for trich or BV at your annual exam; you have to ask for a test specifically.
- If you have trichomoniasis, you will probably be treated with a prescription antibiotic that you take in a single oral dose.
- If you have BV, you will probably be treated with a prescription antibiotic, either orally or in the form of a gel that you insert into your vagina, for at least several days.
- Male partners should also be treated for trichomoniasis; males are not at risk for BV and do not need treatment.
- You should avoid all sexual activity while you are being treated for trich or BV.
- The antibiotics prescribed to treat trich and BV may cause severe nausea and vomiting when mixed with alcohol, so avoid alcohol while you are taking the medications and for three days afterward.
- Both trichomoniasis and BV frequently recur in teenagers.
- If you have BV or trich, ask to be tested for other STDs, such as gonorrhea, chlamydia, syphilis, and HIV.
- The only way to completely prevent trichomoniasis is to abstain from sexual activity. Beyond abstinence, staying in a mutually monogamous relationship, limiting the number of sexual partners, using latex condoms consistently and correctly, avoiding douching, refraining from sharing towels or swimsuits, and getting regular checkups will help protect you. Because it isn't necessarily sexually transmitted, preventing BV is a little trickier, but you can help prevent BV in the same ways.

12

Protect Yourself in Any Situation

Carly, 16, has been dating Scott, 18, for a few months.
They have a great time together seeing movies, going out for dinner, playing miniature golf, and going on other kinds of "dates." Lately, however, Scott has begun to ask Carly for more than just a fun night out. He has been putting pressure on her to have sex, using his age as the main reason why they should do it. He even went as far as to say, "if you don't have sex with me, I will find someone my own age who will." Carly really likes Scott, and she is afraid to lose him if she doesn't give in to having sex. Plus, Scott is leaving for college soon, and Carly fears that if she doesn't have sex with him before he leaves, he will break up with her for an older, more experienced college girl. However, Carly is not sure she's ready for sex. She just turned 16, and the thought of "going all the way" really scares her.

Carly's situation is a common one. Many teenagers date fellow teens a few years older or younger, which can create a mismatch in sexual expectations and desires. It is particularly common for younger girls to date older guys, because teenage girls tend to physically mature earlier than boys. But this physical maturation does not automatically translate to readiness for sex, and it certainly doesn't mean Carly should do something she's not ready for.

In addition, although it is less common, there are also some younger teenage guys who date older girls, which can create a similar conflict over sexual expectations.

And beyond the age discrepancy, there are many other scenarios that put pressure on teenagers to have unwanted sex, from situations where drugs and alcohol are present to long-term relationships. This chapter will help you learn to recognize these situations in advance, so you can be ready for them when they occur. The better prepared you are to handle sexual situations, the better equipped you will be to prevent sexually transmitted diseases (STDs) and other negative consequences of sex.

WANTED VERSUS UNWANTED SEX

Some teenagers feel emotionally and physically ready for sex. If a teen is in a stable, long-term loving relationship, made the decision to have sex ahead of time without feeling pressured by someone else, and is using the appropriate protection, then he or she may have positive physical and emotional consequences from sex.

Many other teens, however, are *not* ready for sex. They may be fearful of what it will feel like and how it will change them, they may be afraid of contracting STDs or becoming pregnant, or they may simply just not be interested in sex yet. Teens who do not want to have sex should not have sex.

Here are some of the reasons teenagers may feel pressured to have sex when they do not really want to:

➤ Many teens feel that everyone else is having sex, so they should too.
➤ Some teens have sex because they think it will keep their partners interested in them and give them the love they crave.
➤ Some teens think having sex will make them feel more like an adult.
➤ Some teens have sex to rebel against their parents.

An especially complicated situation arises when a teen was sexually abused or molested as a child. These types of past experiences can make feelings and decisions about sexuality as a teenager very complex. Research shows that the majority of teenagers who have sex at a very young age also have a history of being abused as children. If you are a teenager who was sexually abused or molested, it is important to share this information with an adult you trust. It is also especially important for you have an ongoing open trusting relationship with an adult throughout adolescence, so you have someone to talk to when issues related to sexuality come up.

Here are some of the potential negative consequences of unwanted sex:

▶ Regret: You never get a second chance to have a first sexual experience, and according to the National Campaign to Prevent Teen and Unplanned Pregnancy, an estimated 63 percent of teenagers under the age of 18 say they wish they would have waited longer to have sex.

▶ STDs: Each year, about 25 percent of sexually active teens have an STD. Of those, over 90 percent do not know they are infected and therefore risk infecting others and suffering long-term health effects, such as infertility.

▶ Unwanted pregnancy: An estimated four out of 10 sexually active teenage girls get pregnant at least once by the time they reach age 20.

Keep in mind that the decision of whether or not to have sex is a very personal one, and you ultimately have the power to make the best decision for yourself in terms of your own values, needs, and priorities. And although it may be easy to lose sight of what you really want due to all the external messages and pressures, if you stay focused and true to yourself, you will make the right choice.

Here is an overview of the specific sexual scenarios you may face, so you can best prepare for them.

LONG-TERM RELATIONSHIPS

The pressure on teenagers to have sex increases for teens in long-term relationships. If you have been dating your girlfriend or boyfriend for an extended period of time, be it a couple of months or a couple of years, people will no doubt start to ask you whether or not you've "done it," and you may feel pressure from your long-term partner to take your relationship to the next level.

Teenaged girls are particularly under pressure to have sex in long-term relationships. A recent U.S. study published in the *Archives of Pediatrics & Adolescent Medicine* showed that teen-aged girls were more likely to feel pressured into sex if they were in a long-term relationship, and nearly 38 percent said they had unwanted sex because they were afraid their boyfriends would be angry if they didn't.

But despite what the media and your peers may have you believe, not all teenagers in long-term relationships are having sex. There-fore, you shouldn't feel pressured to do it simply because you and your partner have committed to each other for an extended period of time. Here are some things you can do to stand your ground or, if you do decide to have sex, to make sure you are doing it as safely as possible:

▶ Talk about it. The time to talk about having sex is *before* you have sex. As part of an intimate, loving, committed relationship, you should talk about sex with your partner long before you make the final decision of whether or not to do it. Don't be shy about bringing up the topic of having sex with your partner, whether you want to tell him or her that you want to have sex or not. Keep the lines of communication as open as possible.

▶ Feel comfortable standing your ground. If your partner loves and respects you, he or she will respect your decision not to have sex. There is nothing wrong with waiting until you know you are completely emotionally and physically ready for sex, so don't feel at all guilty for saying "no." A partner who truly loves you will stay with you, sex or no sex.

▶ Realize that it's OK to change your mind. Just because you have agreed to have sex with your long-term partner in the past doesn't mean you can't say no in the future. You can say no to sex at any time, whether you are simply not in the mood or you have decided to abstain indefinitely.

▶ Stay committed. If both you and your partner agree to have sex, you will be best protected against STDs if you both are committed to having sex only with one another. However, you should keep in mind that it is impossible to be *completely* sure of your partner's sexual and drug use history or to know for sure whether or not your relationship is monogamous, no matter how much you trust him or her. Always practice safe sex, just in case.

▶ Use condoms correctly every time you have sex. You've heard it many times throughout this book: If you are going to have sex, in order to protect yourself from pregnancy and STDs, you must use condoms correctly each and every time you engage in sex. For tips on how to obtain and properly use condoms, see below.

WITH A NEW PARTNER

When you start dating someone new, you are constantly learning things about him or her—what he or she likes to do outside of school, his or her favorite movies, whether he or she prefers chocolate or vanilla ice cream . . . the list is endless. And this "newness" is part of what makes the relationship so exciting. But with a new partner also come new parameters in terms of sexual intercourse, whether you have had sex with other people in the past or not. Together as a couple, the two of you will have to learn each other's views on sex, as well as if or when you will be ready for it in this particular relationship. This takes both maturity and open communication.

Whether or not you choose to have sex—and the amount of time you wait to have sex—with a new partner is a very personal and individual decision. According to a study of 205 14- to 19-year-olds done in San Francisco, the value that young women place on their health and their perceived risk of contracting an STD is positively associated with the amount of time they plan to delay intercourse with a new partner. In other words, in general, the more you value your health and protection from STDs, the longer you will wait to have sex with a new boyfriend or girlfriend . . . if you decide to have sex at all.

The best thing you can do as you enter a new relationship is to have a clear idea of what *you* want in terms of intimacy and sexual intercourse. If you know what you want, you will be able to clearly communicate your needs and desires to your partner early in the relationship, so you won't feel pressured or confused by a surprise request for sex.

Beyond that, you should ask your new partner about his or her sexual history and whether or not he or she has been tested for STDs. You have every right to know what you could be at risk for, even if you are having safe sex. (Remember: Although they lower your risk significantly, condoms do not provide 100 percent protection against any STDs). Also keep in mind that it is impossible to be *completely* sure of your new partner's sexual and drug use history, even if you think he or she is being totally honest with you. Always practice safe sex, just in case.

And remember that you can change your mind any time. Just because you don't feel ready for sex two months into a new relationship doesn't mean you won't be ready two years later. Just like relationships grow and evolve, so do feelings about sex and intimacy.

IN SITUATIONS WHERE DRUGS OR ALCOHOL ARE PRESENT

Drugs and alcohol impair your judgment, making you more likely to engage in risky sexual behaviors that put you at risk for pregnancy and STDs. You've probably heard the term "beer goggles," and although it is clever, it is also true. You become less selective about what you do sexually—and who you do it with—when you drink or use drugs.

In fact, it's estimated that teens age 15 and older who use drugs are five times more likely to have sex than teens who don't use drugs, and according to the National Campaign to Prevent Teen and Unplanned Pregnancy, more than one-third of sexually active teens and young adults age 15 to 24 say that alcohol or drugs affected their decision to do something sexual. Under the influence, you may do something you really regret . . . something that affects you for the rest of your life. Specifically, drugs and alcohol put you at an increased risk for the following:

▸ Unwanted sex: Teens are more likely to engage in unwanted sex while high on drugs and/or alcohol, because impaired judgment can make them falsely think they want to have sex.

▸ Unprotected sex: Studies have shown that teenagers are less likely to use condoms—or use them correctly—when they have sex after drinking alcohol or using drugs than when they do it sober, placing them at an increased risk of HIV/AIDS, STDs, and pregnancy.

▸ Sexual assault: Teenagers are more likely to become both the victims and perpetrators of sexual assault when they are under the influence of drugs and/or alcohol. Remember: It is against the law to have any kind of sexual contact with a person who is incapacitated due to the use of drugs or alcohol.

▸ STDs: Because teenagers who have sex under the influence of drugs and/or alcohol are less likely to use condoms, they have an increased risk for STDs. One study showed that 60 percent of teenage girls and young women who were infected with an STD reported that they were under the influence of alcohol at the time they had sex with the infected person.

▸ HIV/AIDS: Drugs and alcohol make teenagers more likely to have unprotected sex and thus more likely to contract HIV/AIDS. Intravenous drug use is a risk factor for HIV/AIDS as well.

▸ Unwanted pregnancy: Teenagers who have sex after taking drugs or drinking alcohol are less concerned with using birth control, which increases the likelihood of unwanted pregnancy.

And if these potential consequences of sex under the influence of drugs or alcohol aren't sobering enough, what's even scarier is that you may not even remember what you did—or who you did it with—the next morning.

To avoid the dangerous mixture of drugs and/or alcohol and sex, take the following actions to protect yourself:

> ➤ Just say no. Just like abstaining from sex is the best way to prevent STDs and unwanted pregnancy, abstaining from drugs and alcohol is the best way to keep your wits about you and avoid doing something you regret.
>
> ➤ Don't go it alone. Don't go to a party by yourself, particularly if you know that alcohol will be served there. If you are going to drink, choose one friend in your group to be the designated sober person. Or better yet, volunteer to be the sober person yourself. Having one trusted sober person will help keep the intoxicated people from doing things they regret.
>
> ➤ Watch your drinks. If you are going to drink at a party, never let your drink out of your sight. If you do have to put your drink down, make sure you leave it with someone you know and trust. Never leave your drink unattended or take a drink from someone you don't know. Unattended drinks or drinks from strangers are at risk for being tainted with date rape drugs. If you unknowingly ingest one of these drugs, you will become even more incapacitated—and therefore, much more at risk for unwanted sexual acts—than you would be when sober or under the influence of alcohol alone.
>
> ➤ Talk about sex while you're sober. If you plan to drink alcohol and/or do drugs with your boyfriend, girlfriend, or someone you could become sexually active with, discuss your sexual boundaries *before* you start imbibing. If you both have a clear idea of the other's needs and wants, you will be less likely to violate those wishes once alcohol or drugs enter the picture.

WHEN DEALING WITH A PARTNER WHO DOESN'T WANT TO USE PROTECTION DURING SEX

Ultimately, completely abstaining from sex is the best way to prevent STDs. If you are going to have sex, you should use a condom correctly each and every time. Unprotected sex is *never* a good idea for teenagers. It puts you at risk for pregnancy and STDs.

However, knowing you only want to have protected sex is the easy part; communicating this need and holding fast to it with a partner who is trying to coax you out of using condoms is another thing.

Here are some tips on how to make your stance on protected sex clear:

Get it out in the open. The best time to talk about using condoms is *before* you have sex. As uncomfortable as it may be, you need to talk to your partner about your desire to use condoms long before clothing ever comes off. Having this conversation before things heat up will prevent any potential problems and misunderstandings. Don't be shy about talking to your partner about using protection—this is one of the smartest and most important conversations you will have. Plus, talking openly about intimate things such as condom use will bring you closer together as a couple. So don't beat around the bush. When the moment is right, bring it up.

To make it easier, try bringing the topic of condom use up in a relaxed, matter-of-fact kind of way. Try mentioning that you bought some condoms the other day, and offer to bring them along the next time you two get together. You could try asking your partner what his or her favorite condom brand is, or offering to try different brands to find out which ones work best for the two of you.

Overall, be direct. Make it clear to your partner that you won't have sex without a condom. Period. If your partner pushes the issue or threatens to break up with you if you refuse to have unprotected sex, it's time for the two of you to part ways. You shouldn't have sex with someone who doesn't respect you or themselves enough to use protection.

Carry condoms with you. It's traditionally been the male in the relationship's responsibility to buy and carry the condoms, but why should that be? As a female, carrying condoms will empower you to always have safe sex. Best case scenario: Both the male and female partners in a couple carry condoms at all times in case the mood strikes.

Get ready for the excuses. There are classic excuses people use to explain why they do not want to use condoms. If you are ready for these excuses, you will be able to answer quickly with an appropriate and effective response. Here are some of the excuses you might hear:

- ▸ "I don't like sex as much with a condom." You can respond with, "Sorry, but this is the only way I feel comfortable having sex. It will still be good, even with protection." You need to clearly convey the message to your partner that their only two choices are sex with a condom or no sex at all.
- ▸ "I don't know how to use condoms." Because you have learned how to properly use condoms in this book, you can respond with, "I know how, and I can show you; if you want, I can even put it on for you."
- ▸ "I don't have any STDs. Don't you trust me?" You can respond with, "Of course I trust you, but lots of STDs don't produce any symptoms, so you or I may have one and not know it. I would rather be safe, for both of us."
- ▸ "Let's just do it without a condom this once." You can respond with, "It only takes once to get pregnant or contract an STD. I don't feel comfortable having sex unless I know I am protected."
- ▸ "We don't need condoms because you are on the pill (or birth control shot)." You can respond with, "The pill (or shot) is good for preventing pregnancy, but no method of birth control is 100% effective at preventing pregnancy, so using condoms in addition can provide extra pregnancy protection. Plus, it doesn't protect you or me against STDs."
- ▸ "I didn't bring any condoms." If you follow the advice above and carry condoms with you at all times, you can say, "I have some right here."

If you still get resistance from your partner, reassess whether this is a relationship you want. Healthy relationships are built on mutual respect. Someone who is pushing you to do something you do not want to do is not respecting you. Someone who pushes the issue of unprotected sex has likely had unprotected sex in the past, which will put you at an increased risk for STDs. (Remember: not even a condom will provide 100 percent protection)

Use condoms correctly. You've gotten some tips on correct condom use throughout the book, but here is a little refresher course:

➤ Choose latex condoms. Other types of condoms, such as lamb-skin, aren't as effective at preventing STDs. If you are allergic to latex, use polyurethane condoms instead.

➤ Check the expiration date on the package. If they're old, con-doms can dry out and crack, making them useless.

➤ If you want to use lubrication, choose a water-based lubricant. Oil-based lubricants, such as shortening, lotion, petroleum jelly, or baby oil, can break down condoms and make them ineffective.

➤ Open the condom packet carefully with your hands (not your teeth!). You do not want to put holes in it.

➤ Gently roll the condom down until it is completely rolled out. If you accidentally put it on inside out, take it off and start over with a new one.

➤ Choose a condom with a reservoir tip to catch semen after ejaculation. When you put on the condom, gently pinch the top to get rid of trapped air (which can build up pressure and cause the condom to burst).

➤ When you're finished, withdraw the penis from the vagina while holding the condom at the base to prevent it from slip-ping off.

➤ Throw the condom away after it has been used. Do not reuse.

WHEN FACING PRESSURE TO HAVE UNWANTED SEX

These days, teenagers face so much pressure to have sex that some of them may not even know what they want anymore. One recent study published in the *Archives of Pediatrics & Adolescent Medicine* showed that many teenage girls in particular feel they are being pressured into having sex. Of the 279 girls interviewed, 41 percent said they had sex when they didn't want to on at least one occasion. And 10 percent said it was their boyfriends who forced them to have sex. This pressure to have sex seems to occur in a wide range of relationships, from couples who have just met to those who have been dating for a long time; however, the above-mentioned study showed that pres-sure occurred more often in long-term relationships, among partners who had a baby together, when a female felt less sexual control with a partner, when condoms were not frequently used, and when one or both partners used alcohol or drugs.

There is also a lot of buzz in the media over the past few years about teenagers having casual sex or "hooking up" with their friends, which may be used to put even more pressure on teens to engage in sexual activity. "Friends with benefits" is another term for these non-dating relationships. However, it seems these casual relationships may be more hearsay than the norm. In fact, casual

Tips on Where and How to Obtain Condoms

In order to carry condoms—and therefore, to be ready to protect yourself at all times—you have to know where to get them. Here is a list of places you can easily obtain condoms. If you are embarrassed to buy condoms, some of these places, like vending machines in bathrooms, for example, make it easier to buy condoms privately. Some teenagers ask family members, trusted adults, doctors or nurses, or older friends to help them get condoms. Condoms can usually be obtained in the following locations:

▶ Your local drugstore

▶ Convenience stores

▶ Some gas stations

▶ Vending machines in bathrooms

▶ Planned Parenthood and other sexual health clinics (these condoms are usually free)

▶ Supermarkets

▶ Health departments (these condoms will also probably be free)

▶ Your doctor's office (these condoms will also probably be free)

▶ The Internet. Numerous Internet sites sell condoms, including the following:

☐ http://www.DiscountCondomKing.com

☐ http://www.CondomMan.com

☐ http://www.drugstore.com

☐ http://www.AdamEve.com/Condom-Sale

Take the Temptation Away

There are certain situations that make sexual activity especially tempting. If you would like to remain abstinent, the following rules will help you stick to your principles:

➤ Avoid staying home alone with your girlfriend, boyfriend, or someone you are attracted to.

➤ Avoid engaging in affection that goes beyond light kissing.

➤ Avoid attending parties where parents are not home and/or alcohol is served.

➤ Avoid parking your car in a remote spot with your boyfriend or girlfriend.

➤ Avoid sitting in the back row of a movie theater.

sex among teens is not that common. One *USA Today* internal focus group revealed that teenagers say sexual relationships with friends are extreme behaviors, and that most teens value emotional involvement in their sexual (or nonsexual) dating relationships.

Despite its prevalence and the range of forms it takes, pressure from others is no reason to have unwanted sex. Unwanted sex, either in the form of coercion or rape, can harm you both physically and mentally; it has been linked to unwanted pregnancy, STDs, depression, and anxiety disorders.

To push back against the pressures to have unwanted sex, here are some things you can do:

➤ Be clear. Whether you have been dating someone for a few days or a few years, the more open and up-front you are with that person about your desire to put off having sex, the better off you both will be. Do not rely on your partner being able to "read your mind." Communicate clearly by talking, writing, text messaging . . . whatever works for you. Just be clear.

- Stay firm. You should not feel at all hesitant or guilty about your decision to wait to have sex. A partner who truly loves you and values your relationship will respect your wishes.
- Feel free to change your mind. Just because you decided to have sex in the past does not mean you can't become abstinent now. You can say no to sex at any time.
- Talk it out. If you are feeling pressure to have sex or are having a hard time resisting, talk about how you feel with a parent, loved one, or trusted adult. Sometimes just talking about it can release some of the pressure and reinforce your values.

WHEN DEALING WITH MORE EXPERIENCED PARTNERS

It is common for an older teenager or young adult to date a younger teen. For both the older and younger teens, dating someone of a different age can provide exposure to different social groups, and some younger teens think they can learn from older partners. But as Carly's story on page 129 demonstrates, this situation can cause problems when it comes to sexual activity. On average, teens who are dating someone who is at least two years older than they are are twice as likely to engage in sexual activity, and in many cases, that sexual activity may not be wanted. And research has shown that teenage girls who have sex with older partners are at an increased risk of STDs, HIV/AIDS included. So it is safer to date people your own age.

If you are in a relationship with an older, more experienced partner, here are some things you should watch out for. Although these things may not seem to relate directly to sexual activity, they could affect your sexual relationship with this person in the future:

- Inequality. Do you feel like you have an equal say in the relationship when it comes to activities the two of you engage in, people you see, and places you go? Both partners should have an equal say in these things.
- Previous relationships. If you're dating an older teen, he or she may have an extensive history of previous dating and/or sexual partners. Make sure you ask your partner about his or her sexual history and STD status, and realize that you can never be completely sure of whether or not he or she is being honest, so always practice safe sex.

▸ Control issues. If you feel that your partner is trying to control you, be careful. For example, just because your partner is older doesn't mean he or she should have to grant permission for you to spend time with other people. You should still be spending time with friends and family.

▸ Compatibility. If your partner is more than a few years older or younger than you, think about whether or not the two of you are really compatible. Do you have fun together and share some of the same interests, like books, music, or movies? If you have very little in common, the relationship is probably doomed.

▸ Your ages and the law. Different states have different laws in terms of age cutoffs, but you should keep in mind that in most states, it is against the law for someone over the age of consent (usually between 16 and 18) to engage in sexual activity with someone who is under the age of consent. Even if the younger person consents to engage in sex or sexual activities, the older person can still be charged with a crime.

In closing, remember that you do not have to think through issues related to having sex on your own. Talking to your parents or other adults you trust can help you sort things through when you're confused about whether or not you should have sex, you suspect you may have an STD as a result of having sex, you are having problems with a sexual relationship, or you need a sounding board on any other matter related to teenage sexuality.

WHAT YOU NEED TO KNOW

▸ Scenarios that can make teenagers feel pressured to have unwanted sex include: long-term relationships, relationship with a new partner, situations where alcohol and/or drugs are present, when dealing with a partner who doesn't want to use protection during sex, and when dealing with a more experienced partner.

▸ Teens face outside pressures to have sex from their partners, friends, and the media, which forces some to have sex for all the wrong reasons.

▸ Some of the potential negative consequences of unwanted sex include regret, STDs, and unwanted pregnancy.

▸ If your partner loves and respects you, he or she will respect your decision of whether or not to have sex.

▸ Just because you have agreed to have sex with your partner in the past doesn't mean you can't say no in the future.

▸ You will be better protected against STDs if you and your partner are in a mutually monogamous relationship. However, you can never be completely sure of your partner's sexual history and faithfulness, so you should always practice safe sex.

▸ You should use condoms correctly each and every time you have sex.

▸ Drugs and alcohol impair your judgment, making you more likely to engage in risky sexual behaviors that put you at risk for unwanted pregnancy and STDs.

▸ Having sex with older partners increases risk of STDs, HIV/ AIDS included.

13

Helping Friends and Family Members Cope with STDs

Katie and Marisa, both 17, have been best friends since second grade. They talk about everything, from boyfriend troubles to school stresses to problems with their parents. And recently, their friendship reached a new depth when Katie shared an embarrassing secret with Marisa: She had a one-night stand with a guy she met at a party and started experiencing burning during urination a few weeks later. After a trip to a local sexual health clinic, Katie's fears were confirmed—she had contracted chlamydia. Being the devoted friend that she is, Marisa wants to do everything she can to offer support and care for Katie.

Even if you have never suffered from an STD yourself, if a friend or family member is currently dealing with one, you—like Marisa—will be affected. And if this friend or loved one approaches you for advice on how to deal with an STD (be it a chronic virus like herpes or human papilloma virus, or a treatable infection like gonorrhea or chlamydia), surely you will want to be prepared with the most helpful and appropriate things to say. This chapter will help you know what to expect and how to help.

HELPING A FRIEND OR FAMILY MEMBER DEAL WITH AN STD DIAGNOSIS

An STD diagnosis can be hard for anyone to face, but it can be particularly difficult for teenagers. Most teens are not yet comfortable with the responsibilities that go along with having sexual intercourse, let alone are they ready to bear the burden of a sexually transmitted infection. That's why as a supportive friend or family member of a teenager newly diagnosed with an STD, you can provide help and comfort.

First, if your friend or loved one suspects that he or she has contracted an STD but doesn't know for sure, encourage him or her to get tested. After all, the only way he or she will get proper treatment is by knowing for sure. Encourage them to go see their doctor. Sexual health clinics offer free and confidential testing. To help your friend or loved one find a clinic nearby, look in the phone book, search on your local online business directory, or check out http://www.plannedparenthood.org.

Next, understand that your friend or family member will likely go through a series of emotional stages following an STD diagnosis. Those feelings may be particularly strong for teens who contracted an STD from a partner whom they thought they could trust, or if the STD is a chronic one that will affect the rest of their lives, such as herpes or HPV. Understanding the specific emotional stages that go along with a diagnosis can help you recognize where your friend or loved one is in the coping process:

Stage one: Denial. Upon hearing of an STD diagnosis, most teenagers first react with shock and defiance. They may think, "No way—this can't be happening to *me.*" If your friend or family member is in this stage, offer to lend an ear if he wants to talk, and encourage him not to have unprotected sex with anyone else until he seeks treatment.

Stage two: Resistance. Once the diagnosis becomes real, your friend or family member may become very motivated to fight the STD. She may be looking for all kinds of remedies, no matter how off-the-wall. At this stage, you can suggest that she attend a support group for teenagers dealing with STDs in order to learn about the latest and most effective treatment options. You can also do some research on her particular STD, or you can point her to places where she can learn more. You can find good STD information online at the Centers for Disease Control and Prevention (http://www.cdc.gov/std), the American Social Health Association (http://www.ashastd.org), or Teenwire.com, an award-winning sexual health Web site for teens.

Stage three: Adjustment. At this point, your friend or family member may be grieving for his previous STD-free self. He may talk to you about becoming abstinent, being more careful about practicing safe sex, or only having sexual intercourse with monogamous partners. If this is the case, you should encourage him to engage in healthy, responsible behaviors that will help prevent STDs in the future.

Stage four: Integration. At this stage, your friend or loved one will have accepted her STD diagnosis, found treatment, and will be moving on. Now is a good time for you to continue to offer your support and your ear whenever she wants to talk.

UNDERSTANDING THE EMOTIONS INVOLVED WITH HAVING AN STD

Your friend or loved one may experience a range of emotions at any of the stages mentioned above, including anger, fear, guilt, stress, and depression. Here's how to help him or her cope with some of them.

Fear. Fear is a particularly common emotion when it comes to STDs—not only do sufferers fear the physical consequences of the infection, they worry about the social repercussions. The best thing you can do to help your friend or loved one through this fear is to help her become more educated on the disease she has contracted. You can do this by conducting some research on your own and passing on your findings to her.

In addition to fearing the physical symptoms of the STD, your friend or loved one may also fear being alone as a result of her diagnosis. But this hardly has to be the case. Many teenagers and adults deal with STD diagnoses every day. To help her realize that she is most certainly not alone, first, remind her that her STD diagnosis does not change who she is as a person, and that she can still lead a healthy, productive, and happy life. You can also encourage her to join an STD support group. STD support groups offer safe places for people to share their fears and emotions about their STDs and find support from others experiencing the same thing. To find a support group, look online, call the National STD Hotline at 1-800-227-8922, or ask your health care professional to recommend local groups.

Stress. An STD diagnosis naturally stirs up feelings of stress, worry, and anxiety, and these emotions can take a real toll on the immune system at a time when it needs to work extra hard to fight the sexually transmitted virus or infection. Encourage your loved one to help manage the stress of his diagnosis with the following:

- Exercise. Regular exercise improves cardiovascular conditioning, helps control weight, and releases stress-relieving chemicals.
- Counseling. A professional counselor can help your friend or loved one deal with the emotional stress of living with an STD.
- Relaxation. Your friend or loved one can try yoga, aromatherapy, massage, or other relaxation techniques to help manage the stress associated with his diagnosis.

Depression. The link between depression and STDs is a bit of a chicken or egg situation. Studies have shown that teenagers who suffer from depression are more likely to engage in risky sexual behavior, and, therefore, to contract STDs. But the distress that an STD diagnosis itself causes leads to depression in some teenagers. If your friend or loved one who has recently been diagnosed with an STD develops symptoms of depression—loss of interest in activities he once loved, weight loss or gain, restlessness, or mental or physical fatigue—urge him to talk to a health care professional about how he is feeling. If it goes untreated, depression in teens can lead to drug and alcohol abuse, problems at school and home, and in severe cases, suicide. Plus, there are a number of effective treatments out there for depression, so there is no reason your friend or loved one should suffer in silence.

Teenagers who have recently been diagnosed with an STD need the love and encouragement of their friends and family members more than ever. Whether it's your best friend, brother, sister, or cousin who has contracted an STD, your comfort and support will help ease the physical and emotional burden.

WHAT YOU NEED TO KNOW

- Even if you have never suffered from an STD yourself, if a friend or family member is currently dealing with one, you too will be affected.
- As a supportive friend or family member of a teenager newly diagnosed with an STD, you can provide help and comfort.
- If your friend or loved one suspects that he or she has contracted an STD but doesn't know for sure, encourage him or her to get tested. To help the person find a sexual health clinic nearby, ask a health care professional or check out http://www.plannedparenthood.org.

➤ Your friend or family member will likely go through a series of emotional stages following an STD diagnosis. Those feelings may be particularly strong for teens who contracted an STD from a partner whom they thought they could trust, or if the STD is a chronic one that will affect the rest of their lives, such as herpes or HPV. The stages are Denial, Resistance, Adjustment, and Integration.

➤ One of the best things you can do to help your friend or loved one is to do some research on her particular STD or point her to places where she can learn more. You can find good STD information online at the Centers for Disease Control and Prevention (http://www.cdc.gov/std), the American Social Health Association (http://www.ashastd.org), or Teenwire. com, an award-winning sexual health Web site for teens.

➤ To help him find support in others with STDs, you can encourage your friend or loved one to join an STD support group. These groups offer safe places for people to share their fears and emotions about their STDs and find support from others experiencing the same thing. To find a support group, look online, call the National STD Hotline at 1-800-227-8922, or ask your health care professional to recommend local groups.

➤ If a friend or loved one who has recently been diagnosed with an STD develops symptoms of depression—loss of interest in activities he once loved, weight loss or gain, restlessness, or mental or physical fatigue—urge him to talk to a health care professional about how he is feeling. If it goes untreated, depression in teens can lead to drug and alcohol abuse, problems at school and home, and in severe cases, suicide. Plus, there are a number of effective treatments out there for depression, so there is no reason your friend or loved one should suffer in silence.

14

Paying for Care

Bob, Emily, and Samantha have several things in common.
Bob, age 16, is really worried that he might have an STD. He was at a party two weeks ago and had sex with an old girlfriend. He had not been expecting to have sex, did not have a condom, and had sex without a condom. Now he feels foolish, and he has many regrets—including drinking too much alcohol and doing something that he would NOT have done had he been sober. For the past two days, Bob has been having burning when he urinates, and today he noticed yellow pus coming from his penis. He knows he needs to go see a doctor or nurse to be checked. Where will he go? How will he pay for the clinic visit? How will he get and pay for medication to cure his infection, which he doesn't know yet is gonorrhea?

Emily, age 17, contracted genital herpes from her boyfriend Bill about a year ago. The couple had been dating for about nine months, and Emily trusted Bill, so she agreed to have unprotected sex with him. Unfortunately, however, Bill has genital herpes, and because he wasn't having an outbreak at the time that he and Emily had intercourse, he thought he couldn't give it to her. But as mentioned earlier in this book, genital herpes is sometimes contagious in between outbreaks, so Emily was infected.

Emily went to a clinic when she had her first herpes outbreak. The doctor explained that herpes is not curable, but he also explained that if Emily had frequent recurrent outbreaks, she could consider going on a daily medication to suppress them. Emily has been having recurring herpes outbreaks, about every two months

149

for the past year, and she is interested in taking the daily medication. Where will she go? How will she pay for the clinic visit? How will she get and pay for medication to reduce the frequency of her herpes outbreaks?

Samantha, age 16, needs a regular checkup before she goes to school in the fall. She has heard that teenage girls who have had sex need to be tested for chlamydia once a year—even if they do not think they could possibly be infected—because the infection can be silent. She has had sex, and she knows she should get this test at her regular checkup. Where will she go? How will she pay for her clinic visit and chlamydia test?

Bob, Emily, and Samantha all need health care. Here are some things that it is helpful for young people to know when it comes to health care coverage.

WHO PAYS FOR HEALTH CARE?

If you have health insurance, when you go to a clinic or hospital, most of the bill is usually paid by your health insurance company. Ask your parents whether or not you have health insurance, and ask them to explain how this works. As you become an adult, you will need to understand how to get and keep health insurance.

Unfortunately, not everyone has health insurance. Emily, for example, does not have health insurance coverage. Her mom—a single mother—recently lost her job, and as a result, she also lost health insurance coverage for herself and her two daughters. So there is no coverage for the doctor visit or the expensive medications necessary to keep Emily's genital herpes under control.

Health care coverage has become a problem not only for Emily and her family but for many other Americans. And for people like Emily who rely on prescription medications to keep chronic conditions under control, the situation is particularly scary.

Thankfully, there are some things Emily's family and other families like hers can do to get the health care coverage that they need for routine health care, STDs, and other conditions.

GENERAL HEALTH CARE COVERAGE

In the United States, health insurance may be available through your parents' job, your job, or your school if you are in college. Many people have to purchase or buy health insurance on their own.

For a variety of reasons, many families are like Emily's these days in that they do not have adequate health care coverage. In some families, the main breadwinner has been laid off. Other families simply can't afford health care coverage, or they have jobs that don't offer it. And other families make too little money to pay for private health insurance, but too much to qualify for state-subsidized coverage. In addition, some families with health insurance cannot afford the high deductibles and co-pays (portions of the fee for services) that currently go along with many insurance plans.

Luckily, most families have options. Every state in the United States has a program specifically for infants, children, and teenagers in need of health insurance coverage called "Insure Kids Now." Insure Kids Now covers prescription medications, doctors' visits, and other necessary medical services for little or no cost. Although the specific eligibility rules vary, most states will cover uninsured children ages 18 or younger whose families earn $34,100 or less per year for a family of four. For more information on Insure Kids Now, or to research whether or not your family is eligible, go to http://www.insurekidsnow.gov or call 1-877-KIDS-NOW.

Another option for you or your family if you are below certain income limits and do not have health insurance is Medicaid. Medicaid is a state-run public health program that covers a variety of health care services. All states' Medicaid programs cover hospital and outpatient care, home health services, and doctor services. However, in some states, Medicaid requires that you pay a co-payment for some services. For more information on Medicaid and to find out whether or not you and your family are eligible, go to the Medicaid Web site at http://www.cms.gov.

IF YOU NEED STD TESTING OR TREATMENT, BUT DO NOT HAVE HEALTH INSURANCE (OR ARE AFRAID TO USE IT)

If you do not have health insurance, going to see a doctor or nurse can be very expensive. Even if you have health insurance, some young people are afraid to use it when they are worried about STDs. This is because using health insurance can create paper trails that let parents know that a young person has been tested or treated for STDs, even when the young person wanted this information to be kept confidential.

STDs are a public health problem, so everyone works together to try to make sure that people with infection get tested and treated. Fortunately, when it comes to testing and treatment for STDs, there are options available beyond those for routine health care. There have been a variety of attempts to make STD-related medical care free or affordable. Many health departments have special STD services, some cities house STD clinics, and teen clinics and Planned Parenthood centers make extra efforts to provide free or subsidized STD testing and treatment. And because of the potential stigma associated with STDs, these attempts include making confidential services available.

PLANNED PARENTHOOD AND OTHER SEXUAL HEALTH CLINICS

These centers are committed to providing free or subsidized reproductive health services, including STD testing and treatment. They also provide confidential adolescent services when requested and permitted based on individual state laws and professional guidelines. These services are available to both insured and uninsured teens. For more information, go to the national Planned Parenthood Web site at http://www.plannedparenthood.org. On the Web site, type in your zip code or call Planned Parenthood's toll-free hotline at 1-800-230-PLAN to find the closest center to you.

THE AMERICAN SOCIAL HEALTH ASSOCIATION

The American Social Health Association (ASHA) is a nonprofit health organization that provides valuable information on STDs. ASHA can help you think through your options for free or low-cost confidential STD testing and treatment, and they can help you find resources in your area.

In addition, ASHA's STD Resource Center Hotline (1-800-227-8922) provides information, materials, and referrals to anyone concerned about STDs. ASHA's communication specialists will answer questions about STD transmission, risk reduction, prevention, testing, and treatment. For more information on ASHA, log onto their Web site at http://www.ashastd.org, or check out their online STD information section at http://www.ashastd.org/learn/learn_overview.cfm.

OTHER PUBLIC HEALTH DEPARTMENTS THAT OFFER STD INFORMATION AND SUPPORT

In addition, many local and state health departments offer free or low-cost confidential STD-related health services. For information on these departments, call the Centers for Disease Control and

Having problems trying to figure out how to get tested or treated for STDs?

➤ Talk to your regular health care provider.

➤ Call your local health department.

➤ Go to a local emergency room.

➤ Call the American Social Health Association STD Resource Center Hotline (1-800-227-8922).

➤ Go to the American Social Health Association Web site at http://www.ashastd.org.

➤ Go to the national Planned Parenthood Web site at http://www.plannedparenthood.org. On the Web site, type in your zip code or call Planned Parenthood's toll-free hotline at 1-800-230-PLAN to find the closest center to you.

➤ Call the Centers for Disease Control and Prevention (CDC)'s toll-free hotline at 1-800-CDC-INFO (1-800-232-4636); (TTY: 1-888-232-6348). Information is available in English and Spanish.

Prevention (CDC)'s toll-free hotline at 1-800-CDC-INFO (1-800-232-4636); (TTY: 1-888-232-6348). Information is available in English and Spanish.

HELPFUL INFORMATION ON COVERAGE FOR MEDICATIONS

As illustrated by Emily's case, in some situations, STD management requires taking medications on a permanent basis. In other cases, medications are necessary in the short term only to help clear a bacterial STD infection. Either way, most STDs require some sort of prescription medication as part of the treatment process. Most public health clinics, Planned Parenthood clinics, STD clinics, and teen clinics have free or very cheap medications to treat STDs. If you have health insurance with prescription coverage, these medications may be paid for by your insurance company. If you do not have insurance with prescription coverage, and you are going to need to buy medication, so be sure to ask your doctor to prescribe the cheapest medication that will work for you (typically called generic drugs). It is also good to know about some other interesting options.

For one, some pharmaceutical companies offer free medications to people who cannot afford them. To apply for these free medications, you will need a note from your doctor that states the reason you need the medication, as well as a statement declaring that your family has no health insurance to cover the medication and inadequate financial resources to pay for the medication out-of-pocket.

To find out which pharmaceutical companies offer free medications, take a look at the individual companies' Web sites or check out the following Web sites to find out which patient assistance programs offer free prescription medications to those in need:

The Free Medicine Foundation
http://www.freemedicinefoundation.com
The Free Medicine Foundation is a volunteer-run program that helps families like Emily's eliminate or significantly lower their prescription medication costs. The program helps members save an average of $890 per year on each medication they take.
The Free Medicine Foundation works by helping people get free medicine directly from pharmaceutical sponsors. If your family currently has no prescription coverage, maxed-out prescription benefits, or a low income, you are eligible to apply. Families who qualify for free medications have incomes ranging from the poverty level to $80,000. However, each sponsored drug has its own eligibility criteria.

The Medicine Program
http://www.themedicineprogram.com
The Medicine Program offers a free discount drug program to large groups and corporations and is available to anyone who wants to try to lower the cost of his or her prescription medications. The program's free prescription card is accepted at more than 35,000 participating pharmacies and can save you up to 60 percent off your prescription medications.

NeedyMeds

http://www.needymeds.com

A database of patient assistance programs, the NeedyMeds program helps people obtain health supplies, medications, and medical equipment. The site was created by Libby Overly, M.Ed., MSW, a former social worker from Alabama, and Richard J. Sagall, M.D., in 1997, and it is constantly being updated with new information. There is also a hard copy available called The NeedyMeds Manual, which contains all the information from the NeedyMeds Web site.

Partnership for Prescription Assistance

(888) 4PPA-NOW [477-2669]

https://www.pparx.org/Intro.php

The Partnership for Prescription Assistance is a group of doctors, community groups, pharmaceutical companies, patient advocacy organizations, and other health care providers that help patients without prescription coverage to get the medications they need. The organization matches people who are eligible for free or subsidized medications with the public and private programs that can help them. Some of the specific organizations involved with the program include the American Academy of Family Physicians, the American Autoimmune Related Diseases Association, the Lupus Foundation of America, The National Alliance for Hispanic Health, the National Association for the Advancement of Colored People (NAACP), and the National Medical Association.

RxAssist

http://www.rxassist.org

RxAssist is a comprehensive database of patient assistance programs run by pharmaceutical programs that helps people who can't afford medications to obtain free medicines. The site also offers articles to help health care professionals and patients find necessary information, relevant news, and practical tools.

MEDICATIONS FROM CANADA

As prescription and health care coverage become more of an issue in the United States, there is more and more buzz about people buying their drugs from Canada. Although the United States government frowns on the practice, partially because there is no way to regulate the Canadian drugs and assure that they are safe, many consumer advocates say Canada is an economical resource for expensive medications. If you and your parents decide to try to buy medications from Canada, make sure you are using a reputable resource. As the practice of buying medications from Canada becomes more popular, there are several states that have developed programs to help their residents obtain Canadian medications safely.

One of these sites is http://www.i-saverx.net, a mail-order pharmacy program that saves residents of Kansas, Illinois, Missouri, Vermont, and Wisconsin money on prescription medications. The governors of these participating states developed the program to help their residents get lower-cost prescription medications from Canada, Ireland, and the United Kingdom.

In addition, the following states have set up programs to help their residents obtain lower-priced prescription medications from other countries. They include the following:

Minnesota: The governor of Minnesota set up a Web site called Minnesota RXConnect online (www.state.mn.us/portal/mn/jsp/home.do?agency = Rx/) to help residents obtain discounted drugs from both Canada and the United Kingdom.

New Hampshire: New Hampshire offers a few different Web sites to help residents find discounted medications abroad, including a link to CanadaDrugs.com. For more information, go to www. egov.nh.gov/medicine%2Dcabinet.

North Dakota: The following Web site provides North Dakota residents with links to Web sites that import discounted medications from abroad: http://www.nd.gov/content.htm?parentCatID = 91&id = Prescription.

WHAT YOU NEED TO KNOW

▶ Many health departments have special STD services, some cities house special STD clinics, and teen clinics and Planned Parenthood Centers make extra efforts to provide free or subsidized confidential STD testing and treatment to teenagers and adults.

▶ If your family doesn't have adequate health insurance coverage and/or a decent prescription plan, there are ways you can obtain both medical care and prescription drugs at a free or lowered cost.

▶ If your family is below a certain income level, you may qualify for Medicaid, a state program that offers health care coverage to those in need.

- ▸ Every state offers a program that provides health insurance to children and teens who need it, and a number of programs offer free or subsidized prescription medications.
- ▸ Some states provide Web sites for their residents that offer advice on how to obtain lower priced medications abroad.

APPENDIX

Associations and Resources

American Academy of Pediatrics
141 Northwest Point Boulevard
Elk Grove Village, IL 60007-1098
(847) 434-4000
http://www.aap.org

American Cancer Society
(800) ACS-2345
http://www.cancer.org

American College of Obstetrics and Gynecology
409 12th Street SW
P.O. Box 96920
Washington, D.C. 20090-6920
(202) 638-5577 or (800) 762-2264
http://www.acog.org

American Liver Foundation (ALF)
75 Maiden Lane
Suite 603
New York, NY 10038
(800) GO-Liver [465-4837] or (888) 4HEP-USA [443-7872]
(212) 483-8179 (fax)
info@liverfoundation.org
http://www.liverfoundation.org

American Social Health Association (ASHA)
P.O. Box 13827
Research Triangle Park, NC 27709-3827
(800) 783-9877
http://www.ashastd.org

**Center on Addiction and Substance Abuse
  (CASA) at Columbia University**
633 Third Avenue, 19th Floor
New York, NY 10017-6706
(212) 841-5200
http://www.casacolumbia.org

Centers for Disease Control and Prevention (CDC)
1600 Clifton Road
Atlanta, GA 30333
(800) CDC-INFO [232-4636]
(888) 232-6348 (TTY)
cdcinfo@cdc.gov
http://www.cdc.gov

Division of STD Prevention (DSTDP)
The Centers for Disease Control and Prevention
dstd@cdc.gov
http://www.cdc.gov/std
http://www.cdc.gov/stds/pubs

Free Medicine Foundation
http://www.freemedicinefoundation.com

Hepatitis B Foundation
700 East Butler Avenue
Doylestown, PA 18901-2697
(215) 489-4900
(215) 489-4920 (fax)
info@hepb.org
http://www.hepb.org

Hepatitis Foundation International (HFI)
504 Blick Drive
Silver Spring, MD 20904-2901
(800) 891-0707 or (301) 622-4200
(301) 622-4702 (fax)
http://www.hepfi.org

Insure Kids Now
U.S. Department of Health and Human Services

(877) KIDS-NOW [543-7669]
http://www.insurekidsnow.gov

International Herpes Alliance
http://www.herpesalliance.org

The Kaiser Family Foundation
2400 Sand Hill Road
Menlo Park, CA 94025
(650) 854-9400
(650) 854-4800 (fax)
http://www.kff.org

Medicaid
Centers for Medicare and Medicaid Services
http://www.cms.hhs.gov/home/medicaid.asp

The Medicine Program
http://www.themedicineprogram.com

National AIDS Hotlines
American Social Health Association
(800) 342-AIDS (English) or (800) 344-7432 (Spanish)

National Cervical Cancer Public Education Campaign
Cervical Cancer Campaign Specialist
230 W. Monroe, Suite 2528
Chicago, IL 60606
(312) 578-1439 or (866) 280-6605
(312) 578-9769 (fax)
info@thegcf.org
http://www.cervicalcancercampaign.org

National HPV and Cervical Cancer Prevention Resource Center
American Social Health Association
http://www.ashastd.org/hpv/hpv_overview.cfm

National Institute of Allergy and Infectious Diseases
NIAID Office of Communications and Government Relations
6610 Rockledge Drive, MSC 6612
Bethesda, MD 20892-6612
(301) 496-5717
http://www.niaid.nih.gov/publications/stds.htm

National Institute on Drug Abuse
6001 Executive Boulevard, Room 5213
Bethesda, MD 20892-9561
(301) 443-1124
(240) 221-4007 (Spanish)
http://www.nida.nih.gov

National Prevention Information Network (NPIN)
The Centers for Disease Control and Prevention
P.O. Box 6003
Rockville, MD 20849-6003
(800) 458-5231
(800) 243-7012 (TTY)
(888) 282-7681 (Fax)
info@cdcnpin.org
http://www.cdcnpin.org

NeedyMeds
http://www.needymeds.com

Office of National Drug Control Policy (ONDCP)
Drug Policy Information Clearinghouse
P.O. Box 6000
Rockville, MD 20849-6000
(800) 666-3332
(301) 519-5212 (fax)
http://www.whitehousedrugpolicy.gov
http://www.freevibe.com
http://www.theantidrug.com

Partnership for Prescription Assistance
(888) 4PPA-NOW [477-2669]
https://www.pparx.org/Intro.php

Planned Parenthood Federation of America
434 West 33rd Street
New York, NY 10001
(800) 230-7526 or (212) 541-7800
(212) 245-1845 (fax)
http://www.plannedparenthood.org

RXAssist
http://www.rxassist.org

Society for Adolescent Medicine
1916 Copper Oaks Circle
Blue Springs, MO 64015
(816) 224-8010
http://www.adolescenthealth.org

GLOSSARY

abortion   Termination of a pregnancy.

abstinence   The act of abstaining (in the case of this book, abstaining from sexual intercourse).

AIDS   Acquired immunodeficiency syndrome. A very serious disease that breaks down the body's immune system, its main defense against illnesses. In short, people with AIDS are vulnerable to many different diseases and infections that healthy people are immune to. Most people develop AIDS about 10 to 15 years after having been first exposed to the HIV virus.

anal sex   Insertion of the penis into the rectum. Anal sex is the sexual activity that carries the highest risk of spreading HIV.

anorectal gonorrhea   A gonorrhea infection that occurs in the rectum.

bacterial vaginosis   A vaginal infection that results from an imbalance of the naturally occurring bacteria in the vagina.

birth control pills   Hormonal pills taken to prevent pregnancy.

cervix   The place where the vagina meets the uterus. The cervix, which means "neck," has thick, strong walls, and its opening is very small, which keeps things such as bacteria and tampons out of the uterus. During labor, however, the cervix can expand to allow a baby to pass out of the uterus and through the vagina.

chancres   Small ulcers one to two centimeters in size that show up in someone who has been infected with syphilis. Chancres usually appear firm, round, sometimes wet, and small, and they are painless. Chancres generally last three to six weeks and heal without treatment.

chlamydia   A sexually transmitted disease caused by the *Chlamydia trachomatis* bacteria. Chlamydia is the most common STD.

clitoris   A small sensitive organ located toward the front of the vulva, where the folds of the labia meet.

crabs   Slang for pubic lice, parasitic insects found in the pubic hair.

dental dam   A small, thin, square piece of latex that acts as a barrier between the genitals or anus and mouth secretions during anal sex. A dental dam offers protection to both partners during oral-vaginal sex on a female or oral-anal sex on a male or female.

Depo-Provera   An injectable hormonal birth control.

douche   A device that inserts a stream of water or cleansing fluid into the vagina for hygiene purposes. In most cases, douching is not necessary and can actually increase risk for certain STDs.

ectopic (or tubal) pregnancy   A pregnancy that involves a fertilized egg that starts developing in the fallopian tube instead of moving to the uterus. This is a dangerous condition that can be deadly to women.

emergency contraception   The prevention of pregnancy after unprotected vaginal intercourse. Emergency contraception may take the form of the "morning after pill," which is similar to the birth control pill but contains higher hormone doses, or an intrauterine device (IUD) inserted by a physician within five days of intercourse.

epididymis   A tube attached to the testicle that helps transport sperm.

expedited partner therapy (EPT)   With EPT, doctors give a patient antibiotics or a prescription for antibiotics to give to all their sexual partners in attempt to avoid spreading chlamydia. EPT is illegal in some states, however, so ask your doctor about whether or not it is an option for you.

fallopian tubes   The tubes that connect the uterus to the ovaries. Each fallopian tube is about four inches long and approximately as wide as a piece of spaghetti. When an egg pops out of one of the ovaries, it enters the fallopian tube at this fringed opening and travels through the tube toward the uterus with the help of tiny hairs called cilia to push it along.

female condom   A thin sheath or pouch worn by a woman during sex. The female condom was approved by the U.S. Food and Drug Administration (FDA) in 1993. It lines the vagina to help prevent pregnancy and STDs. Currently, the FC and FC2 female condoms are the only ones available in the United States.

genital warts   Warts in the moist skin of the genitals or around the anus caused by the human papillomavirus (HPV).

gonorrhea   A sexually transmitted disease caused by the *Neisseria gonorrhoeae* bacteria.

gynecologist   A doctor who specializes in treating diseases of the female reproductive organs.

hepatitis B   A serious and potentially fatal virus that can be spread by activities that some teenagers engage in, such as sex or getting a piercing or tattoo or injecting drugs. Hepatitis B infections can lead to serious complications, such as liver scarring (called cirrhosis) and/or liver cancer.

hepatitis B vaccine   The hepatitis B vaccine effectively prevents infection by the hepatitis B virus, a risk factor for liver cancer; therefore, the vaccine is being called "the first anti-cancer vaccine." The vaccine is given in a three-shot series.

hepatitis D   Once known as the delta virus, hepatitis D (HBD) uses the outside coat of HBV virus in order to infect cells. A chronic HBV infection automatically puts you at an increased risk for HBD. If you become infected with both HBV and HDV, you will be even more likely to develop cirrhosis or liver cancer than someone who has HBV alone.

herpes simplex virus-1   Herpes simplex virus-1 (HSV-1) is the herpes virus that usually causes sores on the lips, mouth, and gums, called fever blisters or cold sores. Both HSV-1 and HSV-2 are incurable and stay with you for life.

herpes simplex virus-2   Herpes simplex virus-2 (HSV-2) is the herpes virus that usually causes genital herpes. Both HSV-1 and HSV-2 are incurable and stay with you for life.

hormonal birth control   Hormonal birth control methods work to prevent the egg from leaving the ovary (ovulation), and they change the mucus in the vagina to make it too thick for sperm to move through. Birth control pills, patches, or Depo-Provera shots, which are all prescribed by a doctor, are forms of hormonal birth control. Although all of these methods prevent pregnancy 99 percent of the time when used properly, they do not prevent STDs.

human immunodeficiency virus (HIV)   The virus that causes AIDS. HIV destroys an important type of defense cell in the immune system called the CD4 helper lymphocyte.

human papillomavirus (HPV)   A viral infection that can cause warts and cancer. HPV is one of the most common STDs in the United States. It is called the human "papillomavirus" because it tends to cause warts, or papillomas, which are noncancerous tumors. HPV warts usually show up on the genital area.

human papillomavirus (HPV) vaccine   A vaccine that protects against four types of HPV, which together cause 70 percent of cervical cancer and 90 percent of genital warts. The FDA recently approved the HPV vaccine for girls and women ages nine to 26. The vaccine consists of three shots given over six months, and it has been tested in more than 11,000 women and found to be both safe and effective. The most common side effect is soreness in the area of the injection.

hymen   A thin sheet of tissue that partially covers the opening of the vagina. There are several activities that can tear the hymen, including inserting a tampon, vigorous exercise, and sexual activity. Most women experience a torn hymen during their first sexual experience. Although the hymen may bleed when it tears, the amount of pain or discomfort seems to vary.

infertility   The inability to get pregnant.

labia   The two pairs of skin flaps that surround the vaginal opening. Labia means "lips."

lactobacillus   A type of bacteria that makes up 95 percent of the bacteria in a healthy vagina. There are several different types of lactobacillus, at least one of which keeps the vagina's pH at a normal level.

latent syphilis   Also called the "hidden" stage of syphilis, the latent stage can last for years; all signs and symptoms cease, but the infection still lives in the body. Many people with syphilis never progress beyond this stage, but about 15 percent will move on to the dangerous late stage of syphilis, which may not show up until 10 to 20 years after the initial infection.

male condom   A barrier method of birth control, male condoms are rolled onto the man's erect penis right before sex. Condoms provide a physical blockade to prevent the sperm from getting to the egg. They are the most effective method for preventing STDs, but they are not as effective as hormonal methods for preventing pregnancy.

monogamy   The practice of having sex with only one partner. When both partners in a couple are monogamous, it is known as "mutual monogamy."

mons pubis   The fleshy area located just above the top of the opening of the vagina.

nits   Pubic lice eggs. Nits are slightly bigger than the period at the end of this sentence, and they are oval and yellowish-white in color. If you have pubic lice, you will notice these nits attached to your pubic hair.

nymphs   After six to 10 days, nits will hatch into baby pubic lice called nymphs. These nymphs look very similar to adult pubic lice, except they are smaller. To survive, nymphs suck on the blood from skin in your pubic region. About seven days after hatching, nymphs mature into adult lice.

oral sex   When one person kisses, licks, and/or sucks the genital area of another person. Unfortunately, oral sex is too often put in the "totally safe" category when it comes to HIV and other sexually transmitted infections when it shouldn't be.

ovaries Two almond-shaped organs about 1.5 to two inches in size that sit to the upper right and left of the uterus. The purpose of the ovaries is to produce, store, and release a woman's eggs into her fallopian tubes through a process called ovulation. In addition to producing eggs, the ovaries also secrete the female sex hormones estrogen and progesterone.

Pap smear Also called cervical screening, a Papanicolaou smear (Pap smear), which can be performed by your gynecologist or regular doctor, will identify unusual or precancerous changes in your cervix.

pediatrician A physician who specializes in the care of infants, children, and adolescents up to age 18.

pelvic inflammatory disease (PID) An infection that can cause damage of the fallopian tubes and increase a woman's risk for ectopic pregnancy and/or infertility. When certain STDs go untreated, such as chlamydia or gonorrhea, they can lead to PID.

penis The external male organ used for urination and sex. The penis consists of three main parts: the root, the body, and the glans penis.

perihepatitis Inflammation around the liver that can result from untreated chlamydia in females. Also called the Fitz-Hugh-Curtis syndrome.

pharyngeal gonorrhea A gonorrheal infection in the throat, which can cause pain with swallowing and redness of the throat and tonsils.

primary syphilis The first stage of syphilis. The first symptom of primary syphilis is usually the appearance of a sore or sores at the initial site of infection, be it the genitals, anus, or mouth. Syphilis is highly contagious at this primary stage. If the proper treatment isn't administered in the primary stage, the infection will progress to the secondary stage in about 25 percent of untreated people.

proctitis An infection of the lining of the rectum that causes rectal pain and a mucus discharge.

prostate gland A walnut-sized gland that surrounds the urethra and lies just below the bladder. Together with the seminal vesicles, the prostate produces a fluid that protects and nourishes the sperm, called the prostatic fluid. This fluid makes up most of the volume of semen.

prostatitis Inflammation of the prostate that causes pain during or after sex, painful urination, lower back pain, fever, and chills.

pubic lice Parasitic insects found in the pubic hair that spread via sexual contact.

Reiter's syndrome   A condition that consists of knee, toe, or ankle swelling, genital sores, burning during urination, and burning, redness, and/or blurred vision in the eye that can result from untreated chlamydia. Reiter's syndrome is more common in men, but it can also occur in women.

scrotum   The thin sac comprised of skin and muscle that contains the testicles. The scrotum holds the testicles slightly away from the body, which keeps them cooler than the normal body temperature and allows for optimal sperm production.

secondary syphilis   The second stage of syphilis. Symptoms of secondary syphilis may include a skin rash and lesions on the mucous membranes, such as the vagina, perineum area between the genitals and the anus, or mouth. Syphilis is still very contagious during the secondary stage.

sexual intercourse   Heterosexual intercourse that involves penetration of the vagina by the erect penis.

sexually transmitted disease (STD)   A disease or infection that spreads through sexual contact.

spermicide   A contraceptive agent that kills sperm. Spermicides can take the form of foams, jellies, and suppositories.

squamous intraepithelial lesions (SILs)   Invisible lesions caused by HPV. SILs can cover the cervix and require a special instrument called a colposcope to be seen. High-risk types of HPV can cause SIL, which can lead to cervical cancer.

syphilis   An STD caused by the *Treponema pallidum* bacterium, a type of very small bacteria called a spirochete, which is shaped like a corkscrew or spiral. There are a few different stages of syphilis—primary, secondary, latent, and late (tertiary). If any one stage of syphilis goes untreated, it may move to the next subsequent stage.

tertiary syphilis   Also called late-stage syphilis. In the tertiary stage of syphilis, the spirochete bacterium spreads all over the body, affecting multiple organs and systems. The damage caused by the infection can be severe enough to lead to death.

testes/testicles   Two oval-shaped organs that produce sperm (the male sex cell) and testosterone (the male sex hormone). Their size depends on where an adolescent boy is in puberty. Sperm develop in the testes, and tubes attached to the testes called the epididymis and vas deferentia transport them.

trichomoniasis   A single-celled protozoan parasite that causes vaginitis. Infection with trichomonas (trichomoniasis) is the most common curable STD in young sexually active women.

urethra A tube that transports urine from the bladder to the outside of the body in women, and transports urine from the bladder to the outside of the body and transports semen out the tip of the penis in men.

uterus A pear-shaped organ with thick, muscular walls that can expand to accommodate a growing fetus and contract to push a baby out during labor. Also called the womb, the uterus contains some of the strongest muscles in the female body. When a woman isn't pregnant, the uterus is about three inches long and two inches wide.

vagina A hollow, muscular tube that extends from the uterus to the vaginal opening. The vagina serves three main purposes: it is where the penis is inserted during sexual intercourse, it is the pathway for a baby during childbirth (also called the birth canal), and it is the route menstrual blood takes out of the body during a woman's menstrual period.

vas deferens and seminal vesicles Parts of the male reproductive anatomy. Once the testicles produce sperm, those sperm travel through a collection area called the epididymis. They then move on to a tube duct called the vas deferens, which joins the seminal vesicles to form what's called the ejaculatory duct. The seminal vesicles, which are located behind the prostate and the bladder, produce a fluid that lubricates the urethra and provides nutrients for the sperm. This fluid, together with other fluids, makes up semen. When a man ejaculates, the muscles surrounding his seminal vesicles contract to push out semen, which contains the sperm.

vulva The external part of the female reproductive anatomy. Located between the legs, the vulva, which means "opening," covers the vagina and other internal reproductive organs.

yeast infection A vaginal infection that results from the overgrowth of yeast.

READ MORE ABOUT IT

Information on STDs and HIV changes regularly. Data for this book was obtained from the following resources.

American Academy of Family Physicians. "Hepatitis B." http://familydoc tor.org/online/famdocen/home/common/infections/hepatitis/032. html (updated June 2007).

American Social Health Association. "Chlamydial infections." http://www.ashastd.org/learn/learn_chlamydia_facts.cfm (accessed October 29, 2008).

American Social Health Association. "Crabs: Fast Facts." http://www.ashastd.org/learn/learn_crabs_facts.cfm (accessed October 29, 2008).

American Social Health Association. "Gonorrhea." http://www.ashastd.org/learn/learn_gonorrhea_fact.cfm (accessed October 29, 2008).

American Social Health Association. "Hepatitis B questions and answers." http://www.ashastd.org/learn/learn_hepatitisB.cfm (accessed October 29, 2008).

American Social Health Association. "Negotiating condom use." http://www.ashastd.org/condom/condom_negotiation.cfm (accessed October 29, 2008).

American Social Health Association. "Updates from the 2008 National STD Prevention Conference." http://www.ashastd.org/news/news_pressreleases_STDConference2008.cfm (posted March 18, 2008).

AVERT. "AIDS, Sex, and Teens." http://www.avert.org/young.htm (updated September 1, 2008).

AVERT. "The Female Condom." http://www.avert.org/femcond.htm (updated September 19, 2008).

Blythe, M. J., J. D. Fortenberry, M. Temkit, W. Tu, and D. P. Orr. "Incidence and Correlates of Unwanted Sex in Relationships of Middle and Late Adolescent Women." *Archives of Pediatrics and Adolescent Medicine* 160 (2006).

Brown, Nancy L. "HIV infection and teens." Healthline.com. http://www.healthline.com/blogs/teen_health/2006/11/hiv-infection-and-teens.html (posted November 21, 2006).

Centers for Disease Control and Prevention. "Bacterial Vaginosis: CDC Fact Sheet." http://www.cdc.gov/STD/BV/STDFact-Bacterial-Vaginosis.htm (updated February 22, 2008).

Centers for Disease Control and Prevention. "Chlamydia fact sheet—CDC." http://www.cdc.gov/std/Chlamydia/STDFact-Chlamydia.htm (updated December 20, 2007).

Centers for Disease Control and Prevention. "Chlamydia." http://www.cdc.gov/std/chlamydia (updated October 16, 2008).

Centers for Disease Control and Prevention. "Genital herpes: The facts." http://www.cdc.gov/std/Herpes/the-facts/default.htm (updated April 22, 2008).

Centers for Disease Control and Prevention. "Genital HPV infection—CDC Fact Sheet." http://www.cdc.gov/std/HPV/STDFact-HPV.htm (updated April 10, 2008).

Centers for Disease Control and Prevention. "Gonorrhea." http://www.cdc.gov/std/gonorrhea (updated June 5, 2008).

Centers for Disease Control and Prevention. "Gonorrhea: CDC Fact Sheet." http://www.cdc.gov/std/gonorrhea/stdfact-gonorrhea.htm (updated February 28, 2008).

Centers for Disease Control and Prevention. "HIV/AIDS among youth." http://www.cdc.gov/hiv/resources/factsheets/youth.htm (updated August 3, 2008).

Centers for Disease Control and Prevention. "HIV/AIDS Surveillance Report, 2007." http://www.cdc.gov/hiv/topics/surveillance/resources/reports/2007report/default.htm (accessed May 1, 2009).

Centers for Disease Control and Prevention. "HPV and men—CDC Fact Sheet." http://www.cdc.gov/std/HPV/STDFact-HPV-and-men.htm (updated April 3, 2008).

Centers for Disease Control and Prevention. "HPV vaccine information for young women." http://www.cdc.gov/std/HPV/STDFact-HPV-vaccine.htm (updated June 2008).

Centers for Disease Control and Prevention. "Pubic lice infestation." http://www.cdc.gov/lice/pubic/index.html (updated May 16, 2008).

Centers for Disease Control and Prevention. "Sexually Transmitted Disease Surveillance, 2007." http://www.cdc.gov/std/stats07/toc.htm (updated January 20, 2009).

Centers for Disease Control and Prevention. "Sexually Transmitted Diseases Treatment Guidelines, 2006." http://www.cdc.gov/std/treatment (updated February 9, 2009).

Centers for Disease Control and Prevention. "Syphilis." http://www.cdc.gov/std/syphilis/default.htm (updated September 29, 2008).

Centers for Disease Control and Prevention. "Syphilis and Men Who Have Sex with Men—CDC Fact Sheet." http://www.cdc.gov/std/syphilis/STDFact-MSM&Syphilis.htm (updated April 8, 2008).

Centers for Disease Control and Prevention. "Surveillance 2006 National Profile: Syphilis." http://www.cdc.gov/std/stats/syphilis.htm (updated November 13, 2007).

Centers for Disease Control and Prevention. "Trichomoniasis-CDC Fact Sheet." http://www.cdc.gov/STD/Trichomonas/STDFact-Trichomoniasis.htm (updated December 19, 2007).

Centers for Disease Control and Prevention. "2008 National STD Prevention Conference: Summaries of Highlighted Research." http://www.cdc.gov/stdconference/2008/media/summaries-11march2008.htm#tues1 (accessed May 1, 2009).

Centers for Disease Control and Prevention. "Viral Hepatitis." http://www.cdc.gov/ncidod/diseases/hepatitis/index.htm (updated June 27, 2008).

Centers for Disease Control and Prevention. "Youth Risk Behavior Surveillance, United States, 2007." http://www.cdc.gov/mmwr/preview/mmwrhtml/ss5704a1.htm (posted June 6, 2008).

Children's Hospital of Philadelphia. "Chlamydia." The Adolescent Initiative. http://www.chop.edu/consumer/jsp/division/generic.jsp?id = 78793 (accessed October 29, 2008).

Children's Hospital of Philadelphia. "Gonorrhea." The Adolescent Initiative. http://www.chop.edu/consumer/jsp/division/generic.jsp?id = 78794. (accessed October 29, 2008).

Children's Hospital of Philadelphia. "A Look at Each Vaccine: Hepatitis B Vaccine." Vaccine Education Center. http://www.chop.edu/consumer/jsp/division/generic.jsp?id = 75730 (posted March 2008).

Coutinho, Stefanie. "Talking to your teens about sex." *Women Today Magazine.* http://womentodaymagazine.com/fitnesshealth/teensex.html (accessed October 29, 2008).

Datta, S. D., M. Sternberg, R. E. Johnson, S. Berman, J. R. Papp, G. McQuillan, and H. Weinstock. "Gonorrhea and Chlamydia in the United States among Persons 14 to 39 Years of Age, 1999 to 2002." *Annals of Internal Medicine* 2007.

Egendorf, Lisa. *Sexually Transmitted Diseases.* Farmington Hills, Mich.: Greenhaven Press, 2007.

Endersbe, Julie K. *Teen Sex: Risks and Consequences.* Mankato, Minn.: Capstone Press, 2000.

Hatcher, Robert A., James Trussell, Anita L. Nelson, Willard Cates Jr., Felicia Stewart, and Deborah Kowal. *Contraceptive Technology.* 19th rev. ed. New York: Ardent Media, Inc., 2007.

Hunter, Miranda, and William Hunter. *Staying Safe: A Teen's Guide to Sexually Transmitted Diseases.* Broomall, Pa.: Mason Crest Publishers, 2004.

Jacobs, J. Todd. "Pregnancy prevention for young men and women." The University of Michigan Health System. http://www.med.umich.edu/1libr/wha/wha_pregprev_hhg.htm (updated October 19, 2004).

Jayson, Sharon. "Teens define sex in new ways." *USA Today.* http://www.usatoday.com/news/health/2005-10-18-teens-sex_x.htm (posted October 19, 2005).

Kaisernetwork.org. "Encouraging teens to receive HIV test 'much easier' with guarantee of privacy, editorial says." Medical News Today. http://www.medicalnewstoday.com/articles/94257.php (posted January 17, 2008).

KidsHealth for Parents, the Nemours Foundation. "Are changes in my vaginal discharge OK?" http://kidshealth.org/teen/sexual_health/girls/vdischarge2.html (updated November 2007).

KidsHealth for Parents, the Nemours Foundation. "Chlamydia." http://kidshealth.org/parent/infections/bacterial_viral/chlamydia.html (updated August 2007).

KidsHealth for Parents, the Nemours Foundation. "Hepatitis." http://kidshealth.org/parent/infections/bacterial_viral/hepatitis.html (updated February 2006).

KidsHealth for Parents, the Nemours Foundation. "Pubic lice." http://kidshealth.org/parent/infections/parasitic/pubic_lice.html (updated August 2007).

KidsHealth for Parents, the Nemours Foundation. "Trichomoniasis." http://www.kidshealth.com/parent/infections/std/trichomoniasis.html (updated August 2007).

King, K., P. Holmes, Frederick Sparling, Walter E. Stamm, Peter Piot, Judith N. Wasserheit, Lawrence Corey, Myron S. Cohen, and D. Heather Watts. *Sexually Transmitted Diseases.* 4th ed. New York: McGraw-Hill, 2008.

Klein, Elisa. "Am I Ready?" Teenwire.com. http://www.teenwire.com/infocus/2005//if-20050719p368-sex.php (posted July 19, 2005).

MacLean, R. "Teenagers who think sex is important may wait less time with new partners." *Perspectives on Sexual and Reproductive Health.* July–August 2004. http://findarticles.com/p/articles/mi_m0NNR/is_4_36/ai_n6180334 (accessed October 29, 2008).

Marr, Lisa. *Sexually Transmitted Diseases: A Physician Tells You What You Need to Know.* Baltimore, Md.: Johns Hopkins University Press, 2008.

Mayo Clinic. "Chlamydia." http://www.mayoclinic.com/health/chlamydia/DS00173 (posted April 18, 2007).

Mayo Clinic. "Gonorrhea." http://www.mayoclinic.com/health/ gonorrhea/DS00180 (posted January 12, 2007).

Mayo Clinic. "Hepatitis B." http://www.mayoclinic.com/health/ hepatitis-b/DS00398 (posted October 3, 2008).

Mayo Clinic. "Syphilis." http://www.mayoclinic.com/health/syphilis/ DS00374/DSECTION = 1 (posted October 27, 2006).

McKinley Health Center of the University of Illinois at Urbana-Champaign. "Pubic lice." http://www.mckinley.uiuc.edu/Handouts/pubic_ lice.html (posted January 31, 2008).

The Medical Institute. "Genital herpes." http://www.medinstitute.org/ content.php?name = genitalherpes (posted December 2006).

The Medical Institute. "HPV—Human Papillomavirus." http://www. medinstitute.org/content.php?name = hpv (posted December 2006).

The Medical Institute. "Syphilis." http://www.medinstitute.org/content. php?name = syphilis (posted December 2006).

Medical News Today. "Unwanted sex appears common in some teen relationships." http://www.medicalnewstoday.com/articles/44635. php (posted June 6, 2006).

Medline Plus Medical Encyclopedia, the National Institutes of Health. "Chlamydia." http://www.nlm.nih.gov/medlineplus/ency/ article/001345.htm (updated May 21, 2008).

Medline Plus Medical Encyclopedia, the National Institutes of Health. "Chlamydia infections." http://www.nlm.nih.gov/medlineplus/ chlamydiainfections.html (updated August 13, 2008).

Medline Plus Medical Encyclopedia, the National Institutes of Health. "Gonorrhea." http://www.nlm.nih.gov/medlineplus/gonorrhea.html (updated August 15, 2008).

Medline Plus Medical Encyclopedia, the National Institutes of Health. "Hepatitis B." http://www.nlm.nih.gov/medlineplus/hepatitisb.html (updated October 23, 2008).

Medline Plus Medical Encyclopedia, the National Institutes of Health. "Pubic lice." http://www.nlm.nih.gov/medlineplus/ency/ article/000841.htm (updated September 25, 2008).

Medline Plus Medical Encyclopedia, the National Institutes of Health. "Sexually transmitted diseases." http://www.nlm.nih.gov/ medlineplus/sexuallytransmitteddiseases.html (updated October 22, 2008).

Meeker, Meg. *Your Kids at Risk: How Teen Sex Threatens Our Sons and Daughters.* Washington, D.C.: Regnery Publishing, 2007.

The Merck Manuals. "Gonorrhea." http://www.merck.com/mmhe/sec17/ ch200/ch200c.html (updated February 2003).

Miller, W. C., C. A. Ford, M. Morris, M. D. Handcock, J. L. Schmitz, M. M. Hobbs, M. S. Cohen, K. M. Harris, and J. R. Udry. "Prevalence of Chlamydial and Gonococcal Infections among Young Adults in the United States." *Journal of the American Medical Association* 291 (2004).

National Campaign to Prevent Teen and Unplanned Pregnancy. "Sex and Drugs." http://www.teenpregnancy.org/resources/reading/fact_sheets/drugsondcp.asp (updated 2003).

National Center for HIV/AIDS, Viral Hepatitis, STD, and TB Prevention. "Viral hepatitis B fact sheet." http://www.cdc.gov/hepatitis/HepatitisB.htm (updated July 8, 2008).

National Digestive Diseases Information Clearinghouse of the National Institutes of Health. "What I need to know about hepatitis B." http://digestive.niddk.nih.gov/ddiseases/pubs/hepb_ez (posted December 2006).

National Institute of Allergy and Infectious Diseases. "Chlamydia." http://www3.niaid.nih.gov/topics/chlamydia/default.htm (updated June 4, 2007).

National Institute of Allergy and Infectious Diseases. "Gonorrhea." http://www3.niaid.nih.gov/topics/gonorrhea/default.htm (updated June 4, 2007).

National Institute of Allergy and Infectious Diseases. "Sexually Transmitted Infections." http://www3.niaid.nih.gov/topics/sti (updated July 23, 2008).

The National Institute of Allergy and Infectious Diseases. "Trichomoniasis." http://www3.niaid.nih.gov/topics/trichomoniasis/default.htm (updated October 7, 2008).

National Institute on Drug Abuse for Teens of the U.S. Department of Health and Human Services. "What are HIV and AIDS?" http://teens.drugabuse.gov/facts/facts_hiv1.asp (accessed October 29, 2008).

National Institute on Drug Abuse of the U.S. Department of Health and Human Services. "Should Teens Worry about HIV and AIDS?" http://teens.drugabuse.gov/drnida/drnida_hiv1.asp (accessed October 29, 2008).

National Women's Health Resource Center. "Bacterial Vaginosis." http://www.healthywomen.org/healthtopics/bacterialvaginosis/lifestyletips (updated July 20, 2005).

National Women's Health Resource Center. "Chlamydia." http://www.healthywomen.org/healthtopics/chlamydia (updated September 14, 2005).

National Women's Health Resource Center. "Genital Herpes." http://www.healthywomen.org/healthtopics/genitalherpes (updated June 20, 2008).

National Women's Health Resource Center. "Gonorrhea." http://www.healthywomen.org/healthtopics/gonorrhea (updated March 16, 2005).

National Women's Health Resource Center. "Hepatitis." http://www.healthywomen.org/healthtopics/hepatitis (updated May 12, 2005).

National Women's Health Resource Center. "Human papillomavirus." http://www.healthywomen.org/healthtopics/humanpapillomavirus (updated December 14, 2005).

National Women's Health Resource Center. "Trichomoniasis." http://www.healthywomen.org/healthtopics/trichomoniasis (updated June 20, 2008).

North Carolina State University. "Condoms and Safer Sex." http://www.ncsu.edu/health_promotion/Sexuality/condoms.html (accessed October 29, 2008).

Palo Alto Medical Foundation. "Teens and HIV/AIDS." http://www.pamf.org/teen/parents/sex/aids.html (accessed October 29, 2008).

Planned Parenthood. "Guide for Teens and Families." http://www.plannedparenthood.org/health-topics/teens/guide-teens-families-4318.htm (updated August 2, 2007).

Planned Parenthood. "Pubic lice." http://www.plannedparenthood.org/health-topics/stds-hiv-safer-sex/pubic-lice-4279.htm (updated July 24, 2008).

Planned Parenthood. "Teens." http://www.plannedparenthood.org/health-topics/teens-4315.htm (accessed October 29, 2008).

Planned Parenthood. "Teensex? It's Okay to Say: 'No Way!'" http://www.plannedparenthood.org/health-topics/teens/teensex-its-okay-say-no-way-4319.htm (posted November 3, 2003).

Rutgers University. "What If My Partner Doesn't Want to Use Condoms?" http://www.sexetc.org/faq/1049 (accessed October 29, 2008).

Schoeberlein, Deborah. *Everybody: Preventing HIV and Other STDs Among Young Teens.* Aspen, Colo.: RAD Educational Programs, 2000.

TeensHealth, the Nemours Foundation. "About sexually transmitted diseases." http://www.kidshealth.org/teen/sexual_health/stds/std.html (updated March 2007).

TeensHealth, the Nemours Foundation. "Gonorrhea." http://kidshealth.org/teen/sexual_health/stds/std_gonorrhea.html (updated April 2006).

TeensHealth, the Nemours Foundation. "HIV and AIDS." http://www.kidshealth.org/teen/sexual_health/stds/std_hiv.html (updated April 2007).

TeensHealth, the Nemours Foundation. "Pubic Lice (Crabs)." http://kidshealth.org/teen/sexual_health/stds/std_lice.html (updated March 2007).

TeensHealth, the Nemours Foundation. "Syphilis." http://kidshealth.org/teen/sexual_health/stds/std_syphilis.html (updated March 2007).

TeensHealth, the Nemours Foundation. "Talking to your Doctor." http://www.kidshealth.org/teen/your_body/medical_care/talk_doctor.html (updated July 2006).

TeensHealth, the Nemours Foundation. "Talking to your partner about condoms." http://www.kidshealth.org/teen/sexual_health/contraception/talk_about_condoms.html (updated February 2007).

TeensHealth, the Nemours Foundation. "Virginity: A Very Personal Decision." http://www.kidshealth.org/teen/sexual_health/guys/virginity.html (updated April 2008).

University of Maryland Medical Center. "Hepatitis B." http://www.umm.edu/ency/article/000279.htm (updated November 13, 2007).

U.S. Department of Health and Human Services. "Bacterial vaginosis." Womenshealth.gov. http://www.4woman.gov/FAQ/stdbv.htm (updated September 23, 2008).

U.S. Department of Health and Human Services. "Gonorrhea." Womenshealth.gov. http://www.womenshealth.gov/faq/stdgonor.htm (updated May 1, 2005).

U.S. Department of Health and Human Services. "Sexually Transmitted Diseases—Updated 2006 (Morbidity and Mortality Weekly Report)." International Publishing, Inc. March 2007.

U.S. Department of Health and Human Services. "Sexually transmitted diseases: Overview." http://www.4women.gov/faq/stdsgen.htm#1 (updated May 1, 2005).

U.S. Department of Health and Human Services and SAMSHA's National Clearinghouse for Alcohol and Drug Information. "Tips for Teens: HIV and AIDS." http://ncadi.samhsa.gov/govpubs/PHD725 (accessed October 29, 2008).

INDEX